DAWN
OVER
INDIA

DAWN
OVER
INDIA

BANKIM CHANDRA CHATTERJEE

TRANSLATED BY

BASANTA KOOMAR ROY

GYAN

Published by

GYAN

Gyan Publishing House
5, Ansari Road
Daryaganj, New Delhi-110002
Phone: 011-47034999, 9811692060
E-mail: books@gyanbooks.com

Distribution Network
gyanbooks.com
India, USA, Canada, UK, Australia

ISBN: 978-93-6780-511-4 (PB)

First Published, 1941

2nd Impression 2024

Printed at: Gyan Press, Delhi.

DAWN OVER INDIA
Author: BANKIM CHANDRA CHATTERJEE AND
BASANTA KOOMAR ROY

Dawn Over India

DAWN OVER INDIA

By

BANKIM CHANDRA CHATTERJI

Translated and Adapted from Bengali

By BASANTA KOOMAR ROY

Author of "Rabindranath Tagore"

MCMXLI : THE DEVIN-ADAIR COMPANY : NEW YORK

To

BENJAMIN FRANKLIN

whose inspiring life read as a child in a Bengali Reader was my first introduction to America—"The land of the free and the home of the brave," and

SRI AUROBINDO GHOSE

who taught *India* how to suffer, sacrifice and die for Independence, this translation is most reverently and gratefully dedicated.

Translator's Introduction

Chakrabath *paribartante dukhanichaw sukhanichaw* are the words of an old Hindu proverb, of which the English version is: Both good fortune and bad fortune ever turn like the wheels of a car. The man who sits on top of the world today is likely to be plunged into the depths tomorrow. But not for long. With the turn of the wheel he is soon on top again.

India herself is today giving eloquent testimony to the truth enshrined in the old proverb. After centuries of political slavery, of social tyranny and of economic exploitation, the wheel of life in India is beginning to revolve again. And in the new awakening of a great nation of more than 380 millions of human souls, this prophetic novel from the pen of Bankim Chandra Chatterji has played a dynamic part. Sixty years have come and gone since it was first published. In India its influence has been steadily progressive with each passing year.

The theme song of this great novel is *Bande Mataram*—Hail Motherland. Today *Bande Mataram* is

India's national anthem, ringing through the length and breadth of the land as a call to duty. It inspires equally the Mahatma Gandhi pacifists and the Aurobindo Ghose revolutionaries. Suffering the most barbarous atrocities in the British jails in India, thousands of Mahatma Gandhi's disciples chant this great song of freedom. And when Aurobindo Ghose's men have stood on the gallows to be hanged for the 'crime' of loving their own country, they have joyously breathed their last with the sacred *Mantram* of *Bande Mataram* on their lips.

True, Mahatma Gandhi's political philosophy, which owes much to the teachings of Thoreau, Tolstoy and Jesus Christ, is not the philosophy of the great novelist, Bankim Chandra Chatterji. Mahatma Gandhi preaches a gospel of pacifism. Chatterji, on the other hand, sets forth the principle of unselfish militancy as taught by Krishna in the *Bhagavat Gita*, the Bible of the Hindus. And Aurobindo Ghose (now a Master Yogi in exile at Pondicherry in French India with whom Miss Margaret Woodrow Wilson and other students from the West are learning the principles of Hindu philosophy) acknowledges Chatterji as his political *guru*. Here are his words: "Of the new spirit which is leading the nation to resurgence and independence, Bankim Chandra Chatterji is the inspirer and the political *guru*. . . . His was the sweetest voice that ever spoke in prose."

Both in India's renaissance and in her revolutionary movement Bankim Chandra Chatterji occupies a unique position. He was born on June 27, 1838, five years after the death of Raja Ram Mohan Roy. This latter is known as the Father of Modern India; he founded the *Brahmo Samaj*, an organization to which Rabindranath Tagore and numerous other progressive men of Bengal belong.

Chatterji was nineteen years of age when India's War of Independence (known in English histories as the Sepoy Mutiny) began. The following year (1858) India lost that war. Chatterji was finishing his studies at the time, and in that same year (1858) was graduated from the University of Calcutta as its first Bachelor of Arts. The British authorities immediately appointed him to the post of Deputy Magistrate.

But the young Chatterji had suffered a shock in the failure of the so-called Sepoy Mutiny. He could not understand how or why the great movement for independence had so ignominiously failed, and in his effort to discover the causes of that failure he set himself to the task of analyzing the great problem of India's political life. Influenced and inspired by the lives and works of three great patriots–Raja Ram Mohan Roy, Iswar Chandra Vidyasagar, and Rani Lakshmi Bai of Jhansi (the Hindu Queen who had led her soldiers against the British during the Mutiny)–he soon recognized the existence of a number of startling facts.

The people of India, he saw, were fast being denationalized by English manners, English customs, English fashions, and English whiskies and brandies. The

British Government had even gone so far as to make the English language the first language in India's schools and colleges, and Bengali and the other languages of India had been officially relegated to a secondary place. Chatterji's soul winced when he perceived that the Hindusthanee who spoke and wrote English was more honored by his own people than the man who spoke and wrote exquisite Bengali, Marathi, or Hindusthani. Wherever he looked he saw educated Hindusthanees frantically jumping on the bandwagon of British culture. And he reached the conclusion that English, an alien tongue, was being used as a powerful solvent in the destruction of the culture of India.

From the moment when he had first learned to think for himself, he had believed that Bengal had been entrusted with a divine destiny—the destiny of ultimately leading all India into a rebirth of freedom. In Chatterji's view this reborn freedom was to include not merely freedom from British rule but also freedom from the iniquities of the caste system, freedom from the prevailing restraints on style in literature, freedom of women from the tyranny of men, freedom of the farmers from the oppressions laid upon them by the wealthy land-holders, and freedom of thought and action from the manifold thraldom that crippled India as a result of man's own ignorance. But if Bengal were ever to realize this noble destiny, she must have a language strong enough for such a titanic mission and she must evolve a literature dynamic enough to enlighten and to inspire the imagination of the entire people of India.

When the young official of the British Government reached this point in his analysis of the deeper sorrows of his country, both the language and the literature of Bengal were in their infancy. India's ancient classical language is Sanskrit, the mother of all Aryan tongues, including Greek, Latin, and their European derivatives. So Chatterji, confronted with the need to give voice to his beloved Bengal's aspirations as a corrective to the pernicious influence of Britain's cultural imperialism, turned his thoughts to the fabulous wealth of the classical Sanskrit. There, if anywhere, he would find justification for the hopes that surged within him in the year 1871. In that year, when Rabindranath Tagore was only ten years of age, Chatterji faced his problem when he wrote: "Bengali literature is feeble and base and utterly worthless, yet has within it what may encourage no small degree of hope for the future."

So at thirty-three years of age he set his skilful hand to the great task of creating a language for Bengal. Driven by the inspiration of his matchless scholarship, he mined the rich veins of classical Sanskrit. Creating new words, casting old phrases into new moulds, using to the full his uncanny genius for the permutation and combination of syllables, he gradually revealed a world of literary beauty never known in India before.

With Chatterji's novels and essays to boast of, with

their compelling beauty and their subtle humor to point to, Bengal became proud of her honorable place in the world of letters. Men nurtured on Shakespeare, Milton and Shelley began to read the works of Kalidas, Bhavabhuti, Chandidas and Vidyapati. Thinkers who had fed on the works of Darwin, Mill and Spencer turned eagerly to the *Upanishads*, the *Puranas* and the *Bhagavat Gita*. Historical students of the Magna Carta struggle, of the times of Oliver Cromwell, of the tragedy of King Charles the First, began to read the tales of Rajasthan. And the devotees of Sir Walter Scott and Bulwer Lytton opened the pages of Bankim Chandra Chatterji's novels. Within India herself a new feeling had been born; millions began to hold their heads up once again, and men began to talk in terms of "our language," "our literature," and "our country."

Today in India the novelist Bankim Chandra Chatterji is known as the Emperor of the literature of Bengal —*Sahitya Samrat*. He is recognized to be unquestionably India's greatest writer of prose, as Rabindranath Tagore is acknowledged to be her greatest lyric poet. In fact, Tagore was Chatterji's literary disciple, owing much to the sympathy and kindness of the great master. When Tagore, at the most critical period of his literary life, was being cruelly judged by his compatriots for the voluptuousness of his youthful love-lyrics, it was Chatterji's sympathy that fortified his spirit and strengthened his soul. Tagore is today honored in all quarters of the globe as India's Nobel Prizeman in literature. It is good to recall how much the full flower of his genius owes to the sympathy of the older writer.

The incident is well worth recalling. There was a wedding party at the Calcutta home of Romesh Chandra Dutt, a literary disciple of Chatterji. The young Tagore was a guest, and Chatterji was the guest of honor. When the party had settled down, Tagore introduced himself to Chatterji and sat at the great man's feet. During the course of the festivities Dutt, himself a power in the world of literature, made a speech in eulogy of Chatterji and placed a garland of flowers around the great novelist's neck. To the surprise of the other guests, Chatterji removed the garland and placed it around the neck of young Tagore. "This garland really belongs to him," he said. "I am the setting sun. He is the sun at the moment of its rising. Romesh, have you read his *Sandhya Sangit?*"

No one was more surprised than Tagore at this act of kindness. Instantly the young poet forgot the storms of adverse criticism that had been beating down upon his head. With the blessing of his literary guru he persisted in his work. It is not too much to say that Chatterji's kindly approval of his work meant at least as much, if not more, to Tagore than the award of the Nobel Prize that was to come to him many years later.

Like all really great men Chatterji was utterly devoid of jealousy. Writers and poets flocked around him, sure of his sympathy and encouragement. Quite often he picked up unknown writers and helped them to give their best to his own great mission of making Bengali a medium for great thoughts and ideals. "The purpose of literature," he once wrote, "is to help toward ultimate perfection in the culture of beauty, and to instill purity into the mind of man by creative thoughts."

In the realization of this ideal, as well as in the general development of literature in Bengal, Chatterji's Bengali magazine, *Bangadarshan*, played an important role. This magazine, by the way, was afterwards edited by Rabindranath Tagore. In its pages Chatterji published his own writings, together with the writings of many other authors, some of them utterly unknown up to the moment of their appearance under his editorial auspices. Here, too, may be found his vibrant essays on literary criticism. Young Bengal was fortunate indeed to have a great literary craftsman functioning as a creative literary critic. In this connection Tagore's words are eloquent:

"Bankim Chandra Chatterji had equal strength in both his literary hands, he kept his one hand engaged in creative work, and the other in guiding others in what not to do. With one hand he lit the fires of literary enlightenment, and with the other he took upon himself to clear the smoke and ashes of ignorance. Bengali literature was able so quickly to attain such a wholesome maturity in so short a time because Chatterji alone took charge both of ideal creative writing and perfect constructive criticism."

But, with his dream of nation-building to guide him, Chatterji could not confine his interests to literature alone. As the dream began to take form and substance he became vitally interested in history, archaeology, sociology, philosophy, politics and science. For the high esteem which modern science enjoys in India today, that land of transcendent philosophy owes much to the memory of Bankim Chandra Chatterji.

It was in the year 1876 that he made his first outstanding contribution to the cause of modern science in India. In that year the Indian Association for the Cultivation of Science was founded by Dr. Mahendra Lal Sircar, an eminent pioneer in India's scientific work. With the purpose of fostering research and of training teachers Dr. Sircar made a public appeal for funds to support his newly-formed association. The appeal proved unsuccessful. Chatterji, however, came to the rescue of Dr. Sircar. Writing in his *Bangadarshan* he championed the cause of Western science in general, taking occasion at the same time to drive home to India the importance of Dr. Sircar's work. The public response was immediate. In less than two months' time the funds for Dr. Sircar's new association were available. It is to be noted that Dr. C. V. Raman, India's Nobel Prizeman in Physics, is partly a product of this Indian Association for the Cultivation of Science.

But while Chatterji's zeal did much for the fostering of the scientific spirit in academic circles in India, it achieved at least as much in the fields of history, sociology, philosophy and politics. His novels breathe history, sociology and politics; and the aura of profound scholarship clings to his writings on Hindu philosophy. No wonder Tagore pays tribute to this great man's amazing versatility: "In poetry, in science, in history, and in philosophy, whenever and in whatever field he was needed, he was ever ready to give the very best from the fulness of his genius. The great mission of his life was to establish, and to leave behind him for posterity to emulate, the model of an ideal in every department of our newly born Bengali literature. Always he ably and gladly responded to the diverse needs of the helpless literature of Bengal."

Chatterji's dream of a new nationalism for India did not die with him. Its translation into terms of national achievement has now become the definite mission of millions of India's Hindus, Mohammedans, and Sikhs, as well of her other millions of Parsees, Jains, and Christians. The man's great achievement for India was that he made patriotism a religion, and his writings have become the gospel of India's struggle for political independence.

Most popular among those writings, most widely read by the masses, and most deeply impregnated by the spirit of his own great love of India is the novel, *Anandamath*, published herewith. In the original Bengali and in translations in many vernaculars it was widely read in India for twenty-four years after its first publication. But its full significance was not universally recognized in India till the year 1905. In that year the then Viceroy of occupied India, Lord Curzon, in an effort to destroy the solidarity of the Bengali people, partitioned the province of Bengal. This act of arbitrary rule proved to be a blessing in disguise. It united India, and the great nationalist movement was born in Bengal in that same year. Chatterji's novel became the inspiration of this revolutionary movement. Not only in Bengal but all over India men dedicated themselves to the task of making Chatterji's dream come true.

One of the first signs of the new movement was the foundation of the National College in Calcutta. Its Principal was Aurobindo Ghose, a Cambridge graduate, who gave up his relatively lucrative position as Principal of Baroda College at one thousand rupees a month to head the new institution at a salary of one hundred rupees a month. He had hardly settled in Calcutta before he launched a new newspaper, *Bande Mataram*, with its slogan printed boldly at the top of the front page: OUR POLICY–INDIA FOR INDIANS. Instantly achieving a tremendous national circulation, this militant newspaper gave a definite direction to India's thought, focusing men's minds on Chatterji's dream of national independence. In the year 1907 the fighting editor issued his *Manifesto on Indian Nationalism*, declaring: "Truth is with us. Justice is with us. Nature is with us. The law of God, which is higher than human law, justifies our action." In the following year (1908) Aurobindo Ghose was arrested for revolutionary activities.

Ghose's lawyer, at the time of his arrest, was C. R. Das, who soon found himself a national figure and was subsequently elected to the Presidency of the Indian National Congress. In the passage of the years the mantle of Das fell upon the shoulders of Subhas Chandra Bose, a Cambridge graduate who was also a graduate of the University of Calcutta. Bose has ably carried aloft the torch handed on from Chatterji. Twice he has been elected President of the Indian National Congress. On the occasion of his second election, in 1939, he even defeated Mahatma Gandhi's own candidate for the position. In and out of jail, in and out of India, Bose carries on Aurobindo Ghose's political work. Like every other revolutionary worker in India today, he acknowledges Chatterji as his guide.

Chatterji up to the moment of his death in 1894, was unalterably opposed to British cultural anomalies in India. Yet, at the same time, he was a profound student of the great heritage of Western culture and a devoted admirer of the best in Western civilization. He regarded the culture of the West and the culture of the East as mutually complementary, and he did his utmost to use the essence of Western culture to fertilize the cultural life of the new India.

This reverence for the best in Western civilization has been inherited by Tagore, among others. Tagore, writing of Chatterji's international spirit, says: "There was the day when Bankim invited both East and West to a veritable festival of union in the pages of his *Bangadarshan*. From that day the literature of Bengal felt the call of time, responded to it, and having thus justified itself, took its place on the road to immortality. Bengali literature has made such wonderful progress because it cut through all the artifical barriers which would have shut it off from communion with world literature, and because it has regulated its growth in such a way as to be able to make its own, naturally and with ease, the science and ideals of the West. . . . Bankim is immortal not only by virtue of the excellence of the great books he wrote, immortal as they are. He is immortal also by reason of the fact that, with the vision of his paramount genius, he has shown how the ideals of East and West can be harmonized for the universal welfare of mankind."

In those words Tagore pays tribute to what Chatterji actually achieved. But Chatterji himself has told us something of the dream on which he focussed his every activity. Here are his words: "The day European science and mechanical skill unite their forces with India's philosophical idealism, then truly will man become a god."

Basanta Koomar Roy

New York City
July 4, 1941

Book 1

Prologue

VAST, very vast was the forest. Huge trees everywhere stood in endless rows. They entwined one another warmly, and danced in joyous waves in the air. Such was the darkness of this forest that even the blinding light of hot summer days was sightless here. No human could ever dare tread on these grounds.

It was midnight. On all sides darkness enveloped the forest. And the darkness within was like the darkness in the womb of the earth. The birds and other creatures were all in deep sleep. A heavy silence seemed to surpass in intensity even the blackness of this forest. On such a night and in such a forest, a human voice startled the silence by saying, "Shall I ever attain my heart's desire?"

When silence returned, no one could ever believe that he had heard a human voice in such a forest! And yet, after a little while, the same voice cried out again, "Shall I ever attain my heart's desire?"

A third time the ocean of silence was thus disturbed when another voice inquired:

"What can you sacrifice to win your heart's desire?"

"My life itself!" was the reply.

"Life is so insignificant that it is the simplest thing for anyone to sacrifice!"

"What more have I? What else can I offer?"

"Devotion! my friend, devotion!" declared the voice from above.

Chapter 1

It was hot at Padachina even for a summer day. In this village were many houses, but not a soul could anywhere be seen. The bazaar was full of shops and the lanes were lined with houses built either of brick or of mud. Every house was quiet. The shops were closed, and no one knew where the shopkeepers had gone. Even the street beggars were absent. The weavers wove no more. The merchants had no business. Charitable persons had nothing to give. Teachers closed their schools. Things had come to such a pass that children were even afraid to cry. The streets were empty. There were no bathers in the river. There were no human beings about the houses, no birds in the trees, no cattle in the pastures. Jackals and dogs morosely prowled in the graveyards and in the crematories.

One great house stood in this village. Its colossal pillars could be seen from a distance. But its doors were closed so tight that it was almost impossible for a breath of air to enter. Within the house a man and his wife sat deeply absorbed in thought. Mahendra Singh and his wife faced famine.

The year before, the crops had been below normal. So rice was dear this year and people had begun to suffer. Then during the rainy season it rained plentifully. The villagers at first looked upon this as a special mercy of God. Shepherds in the pastures sang in joy, and the wives of the farmers began to bother their husbands for silver ornaments. Of a sudden, God frowned again. Not a drop of rain fell during the remaining months of the season. The rice fields dried into straw. Here and there a few farms yielded poor crops, but government agents bought these up for the army.

So people began to starve again. At first they lived on one meal a day. Soon, even that became scarce, and they began to go without any food at all. The crop was tantalizingly scanty, but the government revenue collector sought to advance his personal prestige by increasing the land revenue ten per cent. And in dire misery Bengal shed bitter tears.

Beggars increased in such numbers that charity soon became the most difficult thing to find. Then disease began to flourish. Farmers sold their cattle and their ploughs and ate up the seed grain. Then they sold their homes and farms. For lack of food they soon took to eating leaves of trees, then grass, and when the grass was gone they ate weeds. Individuals of certain castes began to eat cats, dogs and rats. Multitudes fled from their homes, only to die of starvation somewhere else. Those that did not leave home died anyway. Fever, cholera, tuberculosis and smallpox reaped a rich harvest in human lives. Smallpox thrived most, for there was not a home where it did not claim some victims. Who was there to nurse the sick or to treat them? Alas, there were none to bury or to cremate the dead! Even in the wealthiest houses the bodies of men, women and children rotted unto decay.

Mahendra Singh was one of the rich men of the village of Padachina; but rich and poor were alike now. In those days of devastation and distress, all his friends, relatives and servants were gone. Some had run away; others had died. Now only Mahendra Singh, Kalyani, his wife, and their little daughter were alive in the mansion.

Kalyani woke from sleep. She went to the barn and milked the cow. She heated the milk and fed the child with it. Then she fed the cow with hay and water. Upon her return to the mansion Mahendra spoke to her sadly:

"How long, dear Kalyani, how long do you think we can go on this way?"

"Not very long, I am afraid," replied Kalyani. "Just let me carry on as long as I can. And after my death, take yourself and the child into the town."

"If we have to go into the town eventually, then why should you suffer so much now, Kalyani? Come, let us all go to the town together."

"What can we gain by going there now?"

"Yes, perhaps the town, too, is deserted like this and there is no way of living there!"

"We may be able to save our lives if we go to Murshidabad, or to Kassimbazar or Calcutta. We must leave this place by all means."

"But this home of ours is full of treasures accumulated through generations. Robbers will plunder it in our absence."

"If the robbers come to plunder now how can we two ward them off? And who will enjoy the wealth if we lose our lives by staying here? No, let us lock the house carefully. If we live, we shall return to enjoy our wealth again."

"But you are not used to walking, Kalyani. Do you think you will be able to walk all the way? The palanquin bearers are dead. Horses and coachmen all are dead. You know our situation today, my dear Kalyani."

"Please do not worry about me. I shall be able to walk; even all the way to Calcutta, I am sure."

And Kalyani thought within herself, "No harm even if I die on the roadside; my husband and my child will live."

Next morning they took money with them, locked the doors of the mansion, freed the cattle, and set out for Calcutta with their daughter in the arms of her mother. At the start Mahendra said to his wife:

"The road to Calcutta is very dangerous these days. At every step we are apt to encounter bandits. It is not safe to travel unarmed."

Mahendra re-entered the mansion and armed himself with a rifle and ammunition. When Kalyani saw her husband thus armed, she said:

"Now that you have reminded me of weapons, you had better hold the child for a moment. I must arm myself too."

"What are you going to arm yourself with?" inquired Mahendra.

"You will see."

Kalyani entered the house and armed herself with a little box of poison.

It was the hot month of *Jaistha* when the earth is like a furnace. The scorching rays of the sun had set fire to the air. The sky was like a burning canopy of copper. On the road the grains of sand were like flakes of fire. Kalyani was much fatigued. She continued to walk the road with great difficulty, drinking muddy water from drying pools. The child was given to Mahendra. Now and then they rested in the shade of trees covered with green creepers and fragrant flowers. Mahendra was surprised at the endurance of his beloved. Once he went to a pool, soaked a piece of cloth in water, and moistened Kalyani's face, hands and feet. Kalyani felt much refreshed. But they all began gradually to be overcome with hunger. Their own hunger, however, meant little to them; but the hunger and the thirst of the child were more than the father and mother could bear. Yet they continued their journey, swimming, as it were, through waves of fire; and finally at sunset they reached an inn.

Mahendra hoped that at the inn he would be able to nourish his wife and child with food and drink. He was bitterly disappointed; for the inn was deserted. Huge buildings stood empty. There was not a soul around. Sadly Mahendra made his wife and child enter one of the houses, and lie down. Then he came out, and repeatedly shouted for human beings. No one responded. Mahendra entered the house again and said:

"Kalyani, please summon enough courage to stay here alone for a while. I am going to look for cows. By the grace of God, I hope to fetch milk for you both."

He picked up an empty pitcher that was lying in the house; and started out in search of milk to save the lives of his wife and child.

Chapter 2

IN the gloomy and empty house Kalyani was alone with her daughter. She was afraid. There was no human soul near by. She could hear only the cries of dogs and jackals and she felt she had made a grave mistake in allowing her husband to leave her. It would have been so much better, she thought, if she had only endured the pangs of hunger and thirst a little longer. She thought of closing all the doors of the house; but discovered that the doors and the latches were all gone. Then as she was examining the doorways, she saw something like a shadow at the front entrance. It had human form; but did not look like a human being. This frightful shadow of a man that stood at the door was very dark and emaciated, and all but naked.

In an instant the shadow lifted its hand, and with skeletons of long fingers signaled some one towards it. Kalyani was terror-stricken. Another shadow stood beside the first; then another; and then one more. In a few moments a crowd of uncounted shadows silently entered the room. The dark room was as terrifying as a graveyard at night as these ghosts of human beings surrounded Kalyani and her child—the mother almost fainting—and carried them out of the house, across a meadow, and into the jungle.

Mahendra returning to the house after a short while with a pitcher of milk found no one there. Searching desperately for his wife and child, he found no trace of them. Loud and long he shouted the names of his daughter and wife; but no one responded.

Chapter 3

IT was a delightful part of the jungle where the robbers placed Kalyani. But it was dark; and there were no eyes trained enough to appreciate its beauty. Like the nobility of a poor man's heart, so this beauty of the forest was without appreciation. The entire countryside was starving, yet here were flowers whose fragrance lightened the depth of the darkness. The robbers, having placed Kalyani and her child on a clean plot of ground covered with flowers, sat in a circle around their victims. Soon they became involved in a heated discussion of how to dispose of the woman and her child. They had already taken possession of Kalyani's jewelry and one group was busy dividing these ornaments. When the distribution was over, one man barked:

"What can we do with gold and silver? Will some one here give me a handful of rice for this jewel? I am hungry—I'm about to die of hunger! For the last few days I have eaten only leaves from the trees."

"Rice, give us rice," shouted another, "We are all

about to die of hunger. Give us rice, rice. We don't want gold or silver or precious stones. Give us rice, rice."

The leader of the robbers tried to stop them from shouting, but without success. Louder and louder they talked in abusive language. Soon they were about to come to blows. Angrily they pelted the leader with the jewels. The leader fought them, until they all attacked him together and mercilessly beat him. He was so weak and so emaciated with hunger that with but a few blows he fell to the ground, and there died. Then one of the hungry men cried angrily:

"We have been forced to eat the meat of jackals and dogs. Now lest we die of starvation, comrades, let us eat this man."

The entire band shouted with eagerness. One man began to prepare a proper fire for the feast. He gathered dry creepers, wood and straw, and lighted a flame with flint. Soon the growing fire revealed the green branches and the foliage of the surrounding trees–mango, palm, tamarind and date. Here the leaves were almost ablaze with light; there the grass became radiant; yet in a third corner the darkness by contrast became deeper still. The fire was ready. One of the crowd, dragging the dead body by its feet, was about to throw it into the hungry flames when another member of the group shouted:

"Wait, wait a minute! We have decided to live today by eating human flesh. Why eat the dried flesh of this old man? Let us eat the flesh of those we have brought here today. Let us roast the young woman and her baby. Let's eat their tender meat."

"Roast anything," shouted a third, "whatever you want, but be quick about it—I cannot stand this hunger any longer."

They all shouted joyously at this doubly happy idea, and looked eagerly at the spot where Kalyani had been lying with her daughter. But lo! the spot was empty. Neither mother nor daughter was there.

Taking advantage of the quarrel, Kalyani had run away further into the jungle. Infuriated with the escape of their victims the ghostly men shouted furiously, "Catch! Catch!—Kill! Kill! On all sides in the jungle they scattered to search for the mother and the child.

Chapter 4

KALYANI could not find her way in the darkness. The trees, the creepers and the thorns were so thick that she could make little progress. Yet she must escape. Through crowded trees and thorny bushes she waded to get further and further away from the hungry mob. Now and then the child's body, in spite of all the mother's care, was pierced by thorns. The child cried. The cries reached the pursuers and encouraged them the more; and they cried loud for vengeance. Bleeding and exhausted Kalyani staggered on into the jungle. After a while the moon rose in the darkness overhead. Kalyani was hopeful that the robbers could not find her in the dark; that they would search for a while and then stop. But with the rising of the moon even that ray of hope vanished from her heart. With the glory of its light the moon flooded the top of the forest. Even the darkness in the heart of the jungle lost some of its blackness, and now and then rays of light began to peep through openings in the leaves. The higher the moon rose in the sky, the more light penetrated the jungle; and the darkness retreated further and further into the depth of the forest. In her constant effort to hide herself and her child, Kalyani moved always towards the shades of darkness.

Disappointed, the pursuers became furious with anger. They shouted louder and louder, and circled towards Kalyani from all sides. The frightened child cried loudly. Kalyani, feeling herself trapped, ceased her efforts to escape. She sat down on a thornless plot of green, velvety ground under a huge tree. With the child on her lap she prayed:

"My God, O my God, I worship Thee every day. I bow to Thee every day. It was my faith in Thee that enabled me to enter this jungle with my child. Where, where art Thou now?"

Her resignation crushed in her every feeling of hunger, thirst and fear. She was as in a trance. She awakened from it into a realm of luminous inner consciousness, and in that state she heard a singer chant divinely:

"God is great, God is great;
Take refuge in God; in God alone."

This heavenly music seemed to be coming slowly nearer and nearer. At last it paused over her head. Kalyani opened her eyes to see a Mahatma with long white hair and beard, dressed in pure white. She was moved by the sanctity and serenity of this holyman. In her effort to bow at his feet, she fainted and fell to the ground.

Chapter 5

IN this jungle there stood an old structure, surrounded by broken walls. Archaeologists could easily detect that it had first been a Buddhist *vihara*, then a Hindu temple, and then a Mohammedan mosque. Now it seemed to have been finally converted into something else again. It was two-storied; and its compounds were so formidably surrounded by wild trees and creepers that no one could suspect its existence from a little distance, even in broad daylight. In places the broken buildings had been repaired. At a glance one could recognize that human beings still lived in this impregnably dense forest.

Inside a room of the main building a huge log of wood was burning. It was in this room that Kalyani regained her consciousness. She opened her eyes to see the white-haired and white-bearded Mahatma seated beside her. Kalyani looked around with wonder as in a dream. She had not yet regained her memory.

"Mother," said the Mahatma, "this is the temple,

the mosque, the *vihara*, and the *gurdwara* of Mother India. Cast aside all fear from your heart."

At first Kalyani could not realize what was happening. But as memory returned, she bowed in humility at the feet of the Mahatma. He blessed her; fetched a bowl of milk, warmed it over the fire and said:

"Mother, feed your baby with this milk, and drink the rest yourself. I shall then talk with you."

Kalyani was happy indeed to feed her baby.

"Now, do not be at all afraid," said the Mahatma, "I must leave you for a little while." So saying, he disappeared.

Upon his return he found that Kalyani had finished feeding the baby; but she had not drunk any milk herself. In a tone of surprise, he said:

"Mother, I see that you did not drink any milk yourself. I am going out again. I will not return until you drink that milk."

As he was about to go, Kalyani folded her palms in supplication and bowed to him. "Please do not ask me to drink any milk," she said. "I cannot drink milk."

"What objection can you have to drinking it? I am a forest hermit. You are my daughter. What secret can you have that you do not want to tell me? When I saved you from the jungle I found you suffering from hunger and thirst. If you do not drink milk now, how can you expect to live?"

"You are a holyman," said Kalyani with tears in her eyes, "I must tell you. My husband is not fed yet. How can I eat or drink until I know that he is fed?"

"Where is your husband?"

"I do not know. When he went out to look for milk, we were carried away by that famine-stricken mob."

The Mahatma asked question after question in an endeavor to find out who she was, and who her husband might be. Kalyani, according to custom, was unable to utter the name of her husband. But from what she said the Mahatma guessed who she was, and said, "So you are Mahendra's wife, my little mother!"

Kalyani said nothing, but in the modesty of her assent she looked at the floor, and in deep silence put a piece of wood in the fire over which the milk had been heated.

"Please, do as I tell you," said the Mahatma. "Please drink this milk. I shall go to find news of your husband; but I cannot leave this room until you have finished drinking the milk."

"Is there water anywhere?" asked Kalyani.

The Mahatma pointed to a pitcher of water in a corner of the room. Pouring a little on the palm of her hand, Kalyani requested the Mahatma to sanctify it with his touch. When the Mahatma had blessed the water, she drank it and said:

"I have now drunk nectar, Master. Please do not ask me to drink anything else, for I will neither eat nor drink anything until I get news of my husband."

"Mother, please banish all fear from your mind. Stay strictly within these protected walls in safety. I go to find your husband."

Chapter 6

It was late and the moon hung high in the sky. It was not a full moon; so it was not bright. Light, however, had fallen on the vast meadow making a shadow of the darkness. In such a light you could not see the borders of the meadow. Nor could you see what rested there. It was the very abode of fearful, endless loneliness. The highway to Calcutta and Murshidabad passed over it. Nearby was a little hill covered with mango and other trees. The tree-tops swung to and fro, bright in the moonbeams; and their shadows danced joyously on the dark stones below. Mahatma Satya climbed to the top of the hill; and became absorbed, intently listening. The broad meadow was almost soundless. Only now and then could you hear the whisper of leaves.

At a certain point a vast jungle touched the hill. The hill stood at the top; the highway at the bottom; and the jungle in between. A little noise mingled with the murmur of the trees. No one could know the nature of the noise. Satya walked in the direction of the murmur and entered the jungle. There he found rows of men seated amid the dark shadows of the trees. The men were tall, and armed. Here and there their polished equipment shone brightly in the moonlight that filtered through the openings in the branches. Two hundred men were sitting in perfect silence. Satya walked gently into their midst, and made a sign. No one rose and no one uttered a word. Past the files of men he walked, looking at each face. He seemed to be searching for some one. At last he found the man he sought and touched his body by way of command. The man at once stood up. Satya took him aside to a little distance.

This man was young, his face covered with a black beard and moustache. He was strong and handsome, dressed in yellow, the holy color, his body anointed with sacramental sandal paste.

"Bhavan," asked Satya, "have you any information about Mahendra Singh?"

"Mahendra Singh," replied Bhavan, "left his home this morning with his wife and child; and on their way to the Inn—."

"I know what happened at the Inn. Who did that?"

"Perhaps the farmers of the village. Hunger has driven farmers into robbery. These days, who is not a robber? We ourselves robbed to eat today. We deprived the British chief of police of his two *maunds* of rice for our meal."

"I have rescued Mahendra's wife and child," said Satya smiling, "from the hands of the hungry farmers.

I left them at the *Ashram*. Now, I assign you to find Mahendra Singh for his wife and child. Jiban alone will be able to take care of the duties here, and win success."

Bhavan agreed to undertake the duty. Mahatma Satya departed.

Chapter 7

MAHENDRA soon discovered that it would do him no good to sit down at the Inn, wrapped in idle thoughts and apprehensions. He decided to go into the town, and from there to search for his wife and child with the help of government officials. He had not gone far when he found a bullock cart trudging along with a heavy guard of sepoys of the British army of occupation.

The British had long been expert in collecting revenue. At different centers they had their collectors who seized taxes and revenues to be shipped to the treasury of the East India Company in Calcutta. Thousands of men, women and children might die of starvation; yet there must be no cessation in the collection of taxes. This year's collection, however, fell short of expectations. If mother earth refused to yield wealth, humans could not create it. All that could be collected, however, was being shipped at once to the British treasuries in Calcutta.

In those days robberies were so prevalent that the bullock carts bearing the tax money were guarded front and rear by fifty fully armed sepoys with bayonets drawn. Their captain was an Englishman, who rode a horse in the rear. During the daytime the heat was so great that the sepoys were forced to travel by night. Confronted with this procession of the tax-cart and its guards, Mahendra stepped aside. The sepoys, however, approached him. Realizing that it was not the time for quarrels, Mahendra moved to the edge of the jungle.

"Look, there goes a robber!" said a sepoy. When the sepoy saw the rifle in Mahendra's hands, he was all the more convinced of this. He rushed towards Mahendra, shook him by the shoulders, called him thief, struck him, and snatched the rifle away from him. Mahendra, furious with anger, returned a mighty blow. The sepoy reeled from Mahendra's blow and fell unconscious on the road. Three others then grabbed Mahendra, and dragged him forcibly to the English captain, alleging that he had killed a soldier with but one blow. The English captain was smoking his pipe, and feeling the effects of liquor. He said stupidly:

"Catch that villain and marry him."

The sepoys could not understand. How could they marry a male, armed robber! They hoped the captain would, of course, change his order when he might become sober. So they tied Mahendra's hands and feet, and placed him on the bullock cart. Mahendra knew it was useless to exert his strength against such odds. And again, what would he gain by freedom? He was so sad at his separation from his wife and child that he cherished no desire to prolong his life. The sepoys tied Mahendra well and serenely proceeded along the road as before.

Chapter 8

AT Mahatma Satya's command, Bhavan chanted hymns and set out for the Inn where Mahendra Singh should have been and where he expected to gather some news of the missing man. He followed such a route that very soon he, too, faced the sepoys and the tax-cart. He, too, stepped aside as Mahendra had done. But the suspicion of the sepoys was now so aroused that they at once seized Bhavan.

"Why do you treat me so, friends?" asked Bhavan.

"You are a bandit, villain," replied a sepoy.

"Don't you see I am a holyman, in yellow robes? How can I be a robber? Do I look like one?"

"There are many yellow-robed holymen acting as robbers these days." And the sepoy shook Bhavan by the neck.

In the dark Bhavan's eyes flashed with anger. But he controlled himself, and said with much humility: "My Lord, deign to command, and your orders shall be obeyed at once."

The sepoy was pleased with Bhavan's humility, and said: "Carry this load upon your head, villain."

As Bhavan began to walk with a load on his head another sepoy said:

"No, he will run away. Tie him tight in the spot where the other robber lies."

Bhavan was curious to find out who the other man might be. So he dropped the load from his head; and slapped the sepoy when he lifted it back. The sepoy then tied him hand and foot, and threw him beside the other captive. Bhavan recognized Mahendra Singh.

The sepoys became noisy again and the wheels of the cart began singing loud.

"Mahendra Singh, I know you," Bhavan whispered, "and I am here to help you. It is not necessary now that you know who I am. Please do as I tell you; and do it carefully. Place the knot of the rope that ties your hands on the turning wheel of the cart."

Mahendra was surprised beyond words; yet in silence translated Bhavan's suggestion into action. Moving a little in the dark, he pressed the knot against the wheel. The knot was soon cut by the friction. In the same way he freed his feet. Thus freed, he lay quiet on the cart at a whisper from Bhavan, until Bhavan, too, had freed himself. Both kept silent. The sepoys had to pass by the hill from where the Mahatma had reconnoitered the landscape. The moment the sepoys reached the spot, they noticed a man standing on a mound at the foot of the hill.

"There, there is another rogue of a robber,"

shouted the lieutenant, "go and catch him too. We will make him carry some of our things."

A sepoy ran to catch the man, who did not move an inch. The sepoy caught him, and the man said nothing. The sepoy brought him to the lieutenant. Still the man did not utter a word. The lieutenant ordered that a bundle be placed upon the man's head. It was done. The lieutenant turned and walked alongside the moving cart. Just then the sound of a pistol shot was heard. The lieutenant, shot in the head, fell to the road. In a moment he was dead.

A sepoy caught the silent man by his hand and said:

"This bandit has killed the lieutenant."

The man still had a pistol in his hand. He threw down the bundle from his head; and struck the sepoy with the butt end of his pistol. The sepoy's head was fractured, and he could not molest the man any more. As if at a signal, two hundred armed men rushed out of the jungle and surrounded the sepoys with shouts of victory. The sepoys were awaiting the arrival of their English captain. An Englishman never stays drunk when danger comes. The captain, suspecting bandits, had rushed to the cart and at once ordered his sepoys to form themselves into a square. The square formation was instantly executed. Then at the second command the sepoys pointed their rifles. Of a sudden some one snatched the captain's sword away from his belt; and in a second cut off his head. The captain fell headless on the road, and his order to fire remained undelivered. A man, standing on the cart, was waving a blood-stained sword in the air as he shouted:

"Victory, victory! Kill the sepoys, kill the sepoys."

The shouting man was Bhavan.

The sepoys were terror-stricken and helpless for a moment to see their English captain's head so dramatically chopped off. Taking advantage of this hesitation the energetic invading forces killed or wounded many of them. Then they approached the tax-cart and took possession of the boxes full of coins. Defeated and discouraged the remnant of the sepoys scattered in all directions.

The man who had first stood up on the mound and had then taken the leadership in the fight approached Bhavan. They embraced each other affectionately.

"Brother Jiban," Bhavan said, "your vow for national service is blessed indeed."

"Blessed be your name, Bhavan," Jiban said. Then Jiban began making preparations for the removal of the treasure to its proper place. And soon he departed with his attendants for another destination.

Bhavan stood there alone.

Chapter 9

During the fray Mahendra had leaped from the cart, snatched a sword from a sepoy, and was getting ready to attack his captors. But at second thought he felt convinced that these new people were really robbers. They had attacked the sepoys only for money. So he stepped aside, feeling that if he helped the robbers in any way he would have to bear a share of the sin of this hold-up. When the fight was over, he threw the sword aside, and began slowly to walk away. It was then that Bhavan walked towards him, and stood close to him.

"Gentle sir, may I know who you are?" Mahendra inquired.

"It is not necessary for you to know that."

"Yes, I need to know it. I am greatly indebted to you today.

"I did not realize that you had that much sense in you," the other replied. "During the fight you stood aloof with a sword in your hand. You are a wealthy *zamindar*. In consuming rich dishes for breakfast, luncheon and dinner you are second to none. Yet when it comes to doing something useful, you are nothing better than a baboon."

"You were engaged in sin," Mahendra said contemptuously. "This was robbery, pure and simple!"

"It might be robbery. But you cannot deny the fact that we did some good to you; and expect to render further favors."

"Yes, you have indeed done some good to me. But what more can you do for me? And again, it is certainly a meritorious deed not to accept favors from robbers."

"It rests with you to accept or to reject favors from us! But you may come with me if you so desire. I want you to meet your wife and child again."

"What did I hear you say?" Mahendra inquired, quite surprised.

Bhavan said no more, but started walking. Mahendra, of course, followed him, while he thought within himself: "These are strange robbers indeed!"

Chapter 10

IN the beautiful moonlit night Bhavan and Mahendra were walking quietly across a meadow. Mahendra was silent and sad. He was also proudly curious.

Bhavan, on the other hand, suddenly changed himself into a different personality. He was no longer the quiet and grave holyman, nor the heroic warrior—slayer of the English captain. He was no longer the proud chastiser of Mahendra Singh. He seemed to have been uplifted into supreme joyousness by the unique grandeur of the enchanted panorama. He smiled as the ocean smiles at the rising of the moon. He grew jubilant, talkative, and most cordial. He seemed very anxious to talk. In various ways he tried to engage Mahendra in a conversation. When he failed, he sang softly to himself:

"Mother, hail!
Thou with sweet springs flowing,
Thou fair fruits bestowing,
Cool with zephyrs blowing,
Green with corn-crops growing,
Mother, hail!"

Mahendra was astonished to hear such a song from a robber. He was also at a loss to know for whom these sweet attributes were meant; and who this mother was! So he inquired:

"Who is this mother?"

Without replying to this question Bhavan continued singing:

"Thou of the shivering-joyous moon-blanched night,
Thou with fair groups of flowering tree-clumps bright,
Sweetly smiling
Speech beguiling
Pouring bliss and blessing,
Mother, hail!"

"This refers to a country, and not to a mortal mother, I see," Mahendra remarked.

"We recognize no other mother," Bhavan said with feeling. "The Motherland is our only mother. Our Motherland is higher than heaven. Mother India is our mother. We have no other mother. We have no father, no brother, no sister, no wife, no children, no home, no hearth—all we have is the Mother with sweet springs flowing, fair fruits bestowing, cool with zephyrs blowing, green with corn-crops growing—."

Mahendra now understood the real meaning of the song, and he said:

"Then, please, sing the song again."

And Bhavan sang the song that was destined to transform the life of Mahendra Singh.

"Mother, hail!
Thou with sweet springs flowing,
Thou fair fruits bestowing,
Cool with zephyrs blowing,
Green with corn-crops growing,
Mother, hail!

Thou of the shivering-joyous moon-blanched night,
Thou with fair groups of flowering tree-clumps bright,
Sweetly smiling
Speech beguiling
Pouring bliss and blessing,
Mother, hail!

Though now three hundred million voices through thy mouth sonorous shout,
Though twice three hundred million hands hold thy trenchant sword blades out,
Yet with all this power now,
Mother, wherefore powerless thou?
Holder thou of myriad might,
I salute thee, saviour bright,
Thou who dost all foes affright,
Mother, hail!

Thou sole creed and wisdom art,
Thou our very mind and heart,
And the life-breath in our bodies.
Thou as strength in arms of men,
Thou as faith in hearts dost reign.

Himalaya-crested one, rivalless,
Radiant in thy spotlessness,
Thou whose fruits and waters bless,
Mother, hail!

Hail, thou verdant, unbeguiling,
Hail, O decked one, sweetly smiling,
Ever bearing,
Ever rearing,
Mother, hail!" *

Mahendra noticed that his companion was in tears as he sang.

"Who are you all, pray?" Mahendra asked, quite bewildered.

"We are the Children!" Bhavan replied.

"Children! Who are the Children? Whose children are you?"

"We are the Children of Mother India."

"But, the children of Mother India surely do not worship the Mother by theft and robbery. What kind of mother-worship is this?"

"We neither steal nor rob."

"You just robbed a revenue cart."

"That was neither stealing nor robbery. Whose money did we capture?"

"Why, the King's!"

"King's, you say! What right has an English King to the wealth of our land?"

"The share of the King is due to the King."

"The King is no King at all who does not live in this country, and who rules this land with injustice."

"I am afraid one of these days you will be blown from the mouth of an English cannon."

* Translated anonymously, when it was illegal even to utter the word Bande Mataram.

"We have dealt with plenty of the sepoy slaves of the British. We encountered quite a few today, you know."

"You have not faced them yet. Some day you will really know them."

"We are not afraid. A man never dies more than once in one life."

"What is the use of courting death?"

"Mahendra Singh, I have always looked upon you as a heroic man. Now I see you are just like any other habitual consumer of rich dishes. Look here, Mahendra Singh, the serpent crawls on its breast in order to move about. It is the lowest of animals in creation. And yet, if you tread on a snake it raises its head to bite you. But nothing can disturb your criminal composure! Can you find another country on earth outside India where human beings are forced by starvation to live on grass? Here in India famine-stricken people today are eating creepers, ant-hills, jackals, dogs and even human flesh! And the British are shipping our wealth to their treasuries in Calcutta; and from there that wealth is to be shipped again to England. There is no hope for India until we drive the British out. Only then will the Motherland live again."

"How do you expect to drive them out?"

"By sheer force of arms."

"Perhaps you expect to drive them out all alone—with a slap of your hand, I daresay."

Bhavan sang:

"Though now three hundred million voices through
thy mouth sonorous shout,
Though twice three hundred million hands hold thy
trenchant sword-blades out,
Yet with all this power now,
Mother, wherefore powerless thou?
Holder thou of myriad might,
I salute thee, saviour bright,
Thou who dost all foes afright,
Mother, hail!"

"But you are alone, I see."

"You just saw two hundred more of us."

"Are they all Children too?"

"They are all Children. Yes, most decidedly."

"How many more are you?"

"Thousands upon thousands, and we expect to increase our number steadily."

"Even if you have ten or twenty thousand, you cannot expect to drive the British out of India," Mahendra said.

"How many British soldiers were there under Clive at the battle of Plassey?"

"When it comes to warfare, there is a world of difference between the British and the people of India."

"You do not fight these days with mere physical strength. The bullet does not travel faster nor further because a stronger man fires a rifle."

"Then what makes this difference between the British and the Indian soldier?"

"Because the British soldier would never run away

even to save his life. The Indian soldier runs away when he begins to perspire; he seeks cold drinks. The Englishman surpasses the Indian in tenacity. He never abandons his duty before he finishes it. Then consider the question of courage: A cannon ball falls only on one spot. But a whole company of Indian soldiers would run away if one single cannon ball fell among them. On the other hand, British soldiers would not run away even if dozens of cannon balls should fall in their midst."

"Do you think you Children have acquired these virtues?"

"No, because virtues like these cannot be plucked from trees like ripe fruit. We have to acquire them by patient practice and unyielding perseverance."

"What do you practice?"

"We are all ascetics, you see. But our renunciation is only for this practice. When we have mastered all practices, and attained our goal, we shall return to our homes for our duties as householders. We, too, have wives and children at home."

"You have renounced your families. But have you been able to free yourselves from the ties of love and affection?"

"A Child may not tell a lie—nor may we brag. Who can free himself from all the ties of love and affection? The man who claims to do that, never knew what those ties were. We do not pretend to be above all attachment. We simply observe the sanctity of our vows. Would you like to join the order of the Children?"

"I cannot commit myself to anything until I find my wife and child."

"Then come with me, and you will meet your wife and child."

So they both continued to walk. Bhavan sang the *Bande Mataram* again. Since Mahendra was versed in music and was also a good singer, he joined Bhavan in the song. His eyes became bedewed with tears as he sang. He said gently:

"If I do not have to give up my wife and daughter, you may initiate me as a Child."

"He who joins our order," Bhavan said gravely, "must give up everything. If you really wish to join the order, you cannot ever be with your wife and child. Everything will be properly arranged for their sustenance and protection. But it is forbidden for you even to look at their faces until you have attained the goal of your mission."

"Then I do not care to join the order of The Children."

Chapter 11

It was morning. The forest blossomed again with daylight, and began to echo with the music of the birds. On such a joyous morning, and in such a joyous forest and inside the *Ashram* of the Mother, Mahatma Satya sat on a deer skin deep in meditation. Jiban sat near him.

At that moment Bhavan reached the *Ashram* with Mahendra Singh. In absolute silence the Mahatma continued his morning meditation, quite oblivious to the presence of any one near him. The meditation over, both Bhavan and Jiban bowed to the Mahatma and sat beside him in all humility. Mahendra sat beside Bhavan. After a brief period of silence Mahatma Satya took Bhavan away. We do not know what they talked of; but they both soon returned.

"My son," the Mahatma said to Mahendra, "I am much moved by your sorrow. It was only by the grace of God that I was able to save your wife and child yesterday."

The Mahatma then narrated to Mahendra the story of the rescue of his wife and child. After this he said:

"Come with me, Mahendra, I shall now take you to them."

Mahendra, following the Mahatma, soon found himself in a spacious room with a high ceiling. The room was dark, even though the landscape outside was glowing like a diamond in the sun. At first Mahendra could not see what there was in the room. Gradually a picture revealed itself to him. It was a gigantic, imposing, resplendent, yes, almost a living map of India.

"This is our Mother India as she was before the British conquest," the Mahatma said. "Now say *Bande Mataram.*"

"*Bande Mataram,*" Mahendra said with much feeling.

"Now follow me, Mahendra," the Mahatma ordered; and they entered a dark tunnel to emerge into another, even darker room. Only one ray of light entered it, so it was sad and gloomy. There Mahendra saw a map of India in rags and tears. The gloom over this map was beyond description.

"This is what our Mother India is today," the Mahatma said. "She is in the gloom of famine, disease, death, humiliation and destruction."

"Why does a sword hang over Mother India of today?" Mahendra asked.

"Because the British keep India in subjection by the sword. And she can be freed only by the sword. Those that talk of winning India's independence by peaceful means do not know the British, I am sure. Please say *Bande Mataram*."

Mahendra shouted *Bande Mataram*, and bowed low in reverence with tears in his eyes.

"Follow me along this way," the Mahatma said. They went through another dark tunnel and suddenly faced a heavenly light inside another room. The effulgence of the light was radiating from the map of a golden India—bright, beautiful, full of glory and dignity!

"This is our Mother as she is destined to be," the Mahatma said; and he in turn began to chant *Bande Mataram*.

Mahendra was moved. Tears flooded his eyes as he asked:

"When, O Master, when shall we see our Mother India in this garb again—so radiant and so cheerful?"

"Only when all the children of the Motherland shall call her Mother in all sincerity."

"Where are my wife and child?" Mahendra asked quite abruptly.

"Come this way, Mahendra. You will meet them soon."

"I want to see them but once; and then say good-bye to them."

"Why do you want to part from them?"

"I would join your order of The Children to work for the freedom of Mother India."

"Where do you intend to send your wife and child?"

"There is no one at my home," Mahendra said after a moment's thought. "And I have no other place to send them. I do not know where to find a home for them in these dire days of famine and plague."

"You may go out of the *Ashram* the way you came in. At the gate of the *Ashram* you will find your wife and child waiting for you. Kalyani has not eaten a thing so far. You will find food near where they are sitting. Feed Kalyani first, and after that you may do as you please. At this time you will not see any of us any more. If you do not change your mind, I shall appear before you in proper time."

Mahatma Satya mysteriously disappeared. Mahendra, going out of the main building of the *Ashram*, found his wife and child seated in an adjoining pavilion.

The Mahatma, on the other hand, following a winding tunnel soon reached an underground chamber. There both Bhavan and Jiban were counting the coins from the previous night's encounter, and were arranging them in rows. The entire room was full of heaps of gold, silver and copper pieces; and piles of glistening diamonds, pearls and rubies.

"Jiban, I feel that Mahendra will join us," the Mahatma said as he quietly entered the room. "And it will indeed be a blessing if he joins The Children. For then the hoarded wealth of generations which he owns will be dedicated to the service of the Mother. But, do not accept him into the order until he learns to love Mother India with all his heart, mind, body and soul.

"And when you both are through with this work on

hand; then, alternately watch his movements. When the time is ripe, I shall do what is necessary. Meanwhile, protect them all for, just as to punish the wicked is the duty of The Children, to protect the good is also our duty.".

Chapter 12

KALYANI and Mahendra met after much sorrow and much suffering. Kalyani was overcome with joy to find her husband back again; she actually bathed herself in tears of joy. Mahendra sobbed like a child. Sighing, sobbing and moaning, both became busy wiping each other's tears away. But the more they wiped, the more the tears fell. In order to stop the torrents Kalyani asked Mahendra to eat the food left by an attendant of the Mahatma.

In those days of famine it was not possible for anyone to have a sumptuous dinner. But whatever the country had to offer was not difficult for the Children to secure. Their forest was inaccessible to ordinary mortals. In the country around it was difficult to find fruit on the trees, for hungry people ate it at sight. But no one could find the fruits on the trees of this forest of the *Ashram* of the Mother. Thus it was possible for the Mahatma's attendant to secure various fruits and some milk for Mahendra's family. The only property the Children possessed consisted of a herd of cows. At Kalyani's request Mahendra ate a little. Kalyani fed the child with milk; and she drank a little herself. She saved some milk for her daughter's future use. Then the three, tired and worried, took a nap. Upon waking, Mahendra and Kalyani began to discuss their plans for the future. The problem was—where to go?

"We left our home," Kalyani said, "to escape danger; now I know there are greater dangers outside. So let us return home."

That was exactly what Mahendra was wishing for. He thought it would be best to take Kalyani back to their home at Padachina, to leave her and the child in charge of a proper guardian so that he might himself be free to join the Children, and thus whole-heartedly to accept the supremely pure and heavenly duty of service to the Motherland. He readily agreed to Kalyani's suggestion. And so, rested and hopeful, they started walking towards Padachina.

But in this impregnable fortress of forest they were at a loss to find their way. For a long time they roamed and made every possible effort to get out; but they always managed to return to the *Ashram*. They found themselves caught in the meshes of a bewildering labyrinth.

Then Mahendra noticed a hermit who was standing nearby and laughing. Mahendra was angry at the young man's laughter, and said:

"What makes you laugh, young man?"

"How did you happen to enter these forests?" the young hermit inquired with a smile..

"It makes no difference how we entered—we did, that's all," Mahendra said haughtily.

"If you did, then why are you unable to get out?" And the young man laughed again.

"You are laughing at us. Do you know how to get out of here yourself?" Mahendra asked disgustedly.

"Come with me. I will show you the way out. You must have entered these forests with some hermits of the *Ashram*. It is impossible for strangers to know either how to enter or how to get out.

"Are you a Child?"

"Yes, I am one; so come with me. I have been waiting here to show you the way out."

"What is your name, holyman?"

"My name is Dhiren."

So Dhiren led them out of the wilderness. Then he re-entered the forest alone.

Once out of the wilderness they found a sheltered meadow on one side. The public highway ran along the edge of the forest. Eventually they came by a stream that was singing its way through the woods. The water of the stream was as dark as black clouds, and as clear as crystal. On both its banks the stream was shaded by beautiful green trees. Birds of various kinds were singing in the trees; and the music of the birds mingled harmoniously with the music of the stream. The shadow of the trees blended harmoniously with the color of the water. Kalyani's thoughts, too, were darker as they became more intense. Sitting at the foot of a tree on the very edge of the stream, she asked her husband to sit beside her. She transferred the child to her lap; then placing her husband's hands in her own, she sat silent for a while.

"Why do you look so sad now that the danger is over," she said to her husband.

"Kalyani, I no longer belong to my own self," Mahendra said with a sigh, "and I am at a loss to know what to do."

"Why, what has happened?"

"Please listen to all that happened to me after we were parted." And Mahendra narrated the whole story from beginning to end.

"I, too, have suffered much in your absence," Kalyani said. "I don't want to weary you with that sad tale. But this I must tell you. In the midst of such danger, I don't know how I could have fallen fast asleep yesterday, but I did and I dreamt a strange dream. I felt as if for some unearned merit of my own I arrived at a really wonderful place. There was no earthly thing there. It was full of light—light both soothing and caressing. I found no other human there. I saw only radiant forms of light. The place was overpoweringly full of quiet. I could hear only the mute whispers of a distant, very distant music. And the place was delightfully fragrant with the perfume of myriads of roses, jasmine and gardenias. On a blue mountain that was bathed in this supernatural light an illumined form was seated. There were other forms near it. The light was so bright that I could hardly see. But in front of that form I saw a female form most radiant too. A veil of dark cloud surrounded her, so her radiance was a little dimmed. She was sad and emaciated and in tears; and yet, her beauty was beyond words. She pointed towards me and spoke thus to the form above:

" 'There, there she is! It is for her sake that Mahendra hesitates to take refuge unto me.' "

"Just then a flute struck a beautiful tune for a moment; and the supreme form of light said to me:

" 'You had better leave your husband and come unto me. This woman veiled in darkness is the mother of you both. Your husband must serve her whole-heartedly. He cannot serve her properly as long as you stay with him. So come;—come unto me.' "

"I cried and said:

" 'How can I leave my husband?' "

Then the flute sang again and seemed to say:

" 'I am your husband, I am your mother, I am your father, I am your son, and I am your daughter—so come, do come unto me.' "

"I forget what I said in reply; and I woke from sleep."

Kalyani became silent.

Mahendra too was silent with surprise, wonder and fear. Birds sang overhead; nightingales flooded the forest with their intoxicating music; the cooing of the cuckoos reverberated through the entire woodland. The river sang below. The perfume of the flowers was being wafted on the wings of gentle winds. Here and there sunbeams played hide-and-seek with the dark waters of the river. Palm leaves murmured against the winds. Ranges of blue mountains could be seen in the distance. Mahendra and Kalyani sat quietly for a long time.

"What are you thinking of?" Kalyani broke this silence.

"I am wondering what I should do," Mahendra said. "A dream is but an illusion. It rises and falls only in the human mind. It has no reality, it is only a bubble of life; let us go home."

"Please go where duty calls you." And Kalyani transferred the child to the lap of her husband.

"And you—where will you go?" Mahendra asked in agony.

Kalyani hid her face behind her hands and said: "I, too, shall go where my duty has already called me."

"Where is that? And how can you go there?" Mahendra asked, much startled.

Kalyani showed Mahendra the little box of poison.

"What, you want to take poison!"

"Yes, I thought I would take poison, but—"

Kalyani thought in silence. Mahendra continued to look at her face intently. Every moment dragged like a year. As Kalyani did not finish her sentence, Mahendra asked:

"You started to say something, Kalyani. Please tell me what you had on your mind?"

"Yes, I was thinking seriously of taking poison, but I would not wish to enter heaven and leave you and Sukumari behind. No, I cannot die!"

Kalyani dropped the box of poison to the ground;

and soon they both became warmly interested in a discussion of things of the past and the future. In the meantime, the child had picked up the little box of poison, and had begun to play with it. Now she placed it in her left hand, and struck it with her right hand; and again, she would place it in her right hand, and strike it with her left. Then with both her little hands she pulled at the box. Suddenly the box opened by itself, and the pill of poison fell on Mahendra's dress. Sukumari thought that the pill was something else to play with. Throwing aside the box, she quickly picked up the pill of poison and put it into her mouth.

By the merest chance Kalyani saw her daughter put something into her mouth, and noticing the empty box lying on the ground, she cried out:

"I am afraid Sukumari has swallowed poison; I am afraid—"

And she thrust a couple of her fingers into Sukumari's mouth. Sukumari thought that Kalyani was playing with her. So she pressed her teeth tight, and smiled up at her mother. But the pill must have tasted bitter, for Sukumari soon opened her mouth, and the mother pulled the pill out. The pill fell to the ground and the child began to cry.

Kalyani rushed to the river, soaked the border of her *sari* and rushed back to her daughter to wipe her tongue. While she was doing this she asked Mahendra:

"Do you think any of the poison has reached her stomach?"

Parents think of danger to their children rather than

of their own safety. Wherever true love exists, there fear is ever present. Mahendra had not noticed how large the pill originally had been. And yet he examined it and said:

"I am afraid she has swallowed quite a lot."

Kalyani readily believed what her husband said. Then she, too, took the pill in her own hand, and looked at it carefully. Meanwhile, the child began to grow pale from what little of the pill she had swallowed. She became restless, and began to cry bitterly. In a moment she fainted. Kalyani, becoming frantic with fear and distress, said to Mahendra:

"There is nothing more to think about. Here ends the life of Sukumari! I must now follow her, and thus respond to the call of my duty."

And Kalyani wasted not a moment in swallowing the pill of poison.

"Kalyani, O my Kalyani, why did you do that? Why did you do that?" Mahendra cried over and over again.

"Words will only beget words—so this is goodbye," Kalyani said as she fell at her husband's feet.

"Kalyani, why did you do that? You are most cruel, Kalyani, most cruel! Oh why did you do it?"

"I have done well," Kalyani said faintly. "I was afraid that for my sake you might refuse to follow the path of your own duty. I was about to shirk duty myself; and so I lost my child. If I shirk my duty any longer, I might lose you too."

"I could have kept you some place; and I might

have joined you after winning the independence of India—yes, joined you for the complete happiness of my life. Kalyani, you are the whole of my being. Why did you swallow the poison? You have thus cut off the hand that gave me strength to wield the sword for our Mother India. Kalyani, what am I without you? I am nothing—absolutely nothing without you."

"Where could you have taken me?" she asked, "We have no place to go. In this frightful famine and plague we have lost our parents, and all our friends. Who could shelter us now? Where could we go? Where, O where could you take me? I have been a burden to your progress. Death is a happy thing for me. Bless me that I may meet you again in that realm of Light."

Kalyani again bowed at Mahendra's feet. Unable to speak Mahendra cried like a child.

"Who can counteract the will of God?" Kalyani said faintly, but with sweetness and affection. "I have His command to depart; and I cannot stay here on earth even if I want to do it with all my heart. Had I not swallowed poison, some other agency would certainly have killed me. By choosing death this way, and in your presence, I have done well. And it is your duty to fulfill the conditions of your vow with the utmost fidelity. Faithfully with all your body, mind and soul, you must now serve Mother India. Fight for India's freedom with all the forces at your command. This is your path of duty—your *dharma*. Solely through this path salvation awaits you. And in fullness of time, and by virtue of your noble and unselfish deeds, we shall meet again in that Kingdom of Light, and live there together throughout eternity."

Sukumari, on the other hand, was safe for the moment. The small amount of poison she had swallowed was not yet fatal. Mahendra placed Sukumari on Kalyani's lap, and in a flood of tears embraced them both lovingly. Just then one could hear a gentle, but deep voice sing the *Bande Mataram* in the woods. From the very depth of her subconscious self, Kalyani beautifully sang the first line of this hymn to the Mother.

"Kalyani, sing the *Bande Mataram* again," Mahendra begged.

Kalyani sang it again, her voice mingling with the music from the forest. Mahendra was enraptured with the heavenly melody of the song. In prayer he lifted his eyes to God, his only friend left on earth.

Out of the fullness of his heart Mahendra himself began to sing the *Bande Mataram* in the rapturous joy of devotional fervor. He heard this hymn sung all around him, and its melody came to him from every part of the forest. He felt as if the birds on the trees were singing the *Bande Mataram*. He felt as if the stream were singing it. Of a sudden he sat transformed. Mysteriously he rose above all pain and all sorrow. Tears vanished from his eyes. Gently he mingled his music with that of Kalyani and both sang soulfully. The entire forest joined with them in the chant.

Kalyani's voice became fainter and fainter. Still she continued to sing the *Bande Mataram*. Slowly and slowly her voice failed. Then came the moment when she neither spoke nor sang. Her eyes closed. Her body became cold. Mahendra felt that Kalyani had attained heaven.

Then, like an infuriated man, Mahendra repeatedly cried *Bande Mataram* loud enough to shake the forests, to frighten the wild animals in their dens, and to rend the skies above. Some one then embraced him lovingly and began to chant the same song with him. Thus in the infinite forest, at the mercy of the Infinite, and before the body of the dying Kalyani on her journey to the Infinite, two comrades sang from the very bottom of their hearts and from the depth of their souls. The birds and the beasts became quiet again. The forest became a fitting tabernacle for this song of the Mother.

Mahatma Satya sat with Mahendra's head in his lap.

Chapter 13

CALCUTTA, the capital of British occupied India, was seething with excitement. The burning topic of the day was the confiscation of the British revenue cart by the hermit nationalists. The British government at once issued urgent orders for open war against nationalists who disguised themselves as holymen. Soldiers and policemen were dispatched to capture the *sanyasis* at sight.

In those days of famine there were but few real hermits in that part of the country. For the real *sanyasis* lived on alms; and the people were finding it difficult enough to prolong their own lives, not to speak of giving alms. The real *sanyasis* consequently migrated to the places of pilgrimage like Benares and Allahabad. As a camouflage, the Children assumed the yellow robes of the *sanyasis*, changing costumes whenever they felt it necessary. At the very suggestion of trouble they put off their yellow robes, and the hungry sepoy soldiers and policemen then found no *sanyasis* anywhere. So the hunters commandeered food from the kitchens and pantries of the people, and thus half satisfied their hunger. Mahatma Satya was the only one who clung stubbornly to his yellow robe.

Kalyani was still lying under a tree on the bank of the dark and singing stream. Mahendra and Mahatma Satya were in deep embrace, as they continued to pray while their eyes ran with tears. Suddenly and unexpectedly, their prayers were disturbed. An Indian lieutenant of the British army appeared before them with five sepoys. The lieutenant at once grabbed Mahatma Satya's shoulder and said:

"Here, this rogue is a *sanyasi*."

A sepoy at once arrested Mahendra too; for, he reasoned, a companion of a *sanyasi* must also be a *sanyasi*. Another sepoy was about to touch the dead body of Kalyani lying on the grass, but he realized that the dead body of a woman was hardly apt to be a *sanyasini*. So he did not touch Kalyani and similarly he left the child alone. Then the sepoys, without wasting words, tied the hands of their prisoners and marched off with them. The still bodies of Kalyani and Sukumari remained unprotected at the foot of the tree.

Afflicted with harrowing sorrow, and yet inspired with a deep fervor of devotion, Mahendra was almost unconscious. He hardly realized what had happened or what was happening to him. When his hands were bound he did not object. But as he was being dragged a little away from his wife's body, he realized that the Mahatma and he were being marched off as prisoners.

He began to think of his wife and child lying under the tree uncremated. And in a moment the thought came that perhaps they were even then being devoured by wild beasts. With one tremendous jerk he tore the rope that bound his wrists. He kicked the lieutenant so hard that the man fell to the ground. As he was about to attack a sepoy, three others seized and overpowered him. Broken by sorrow, he then addressed Mahatma Satya: "If you had but helped me a little, I could have killed every one of these five villains."

"What strength," said Mahatma Satya, "have I in my old body? I was calling on the One who is the only source of all strength. Do not stand in the way of the inevitable. Rather, let us watch where they take us. God will arrange things properly on all sides."

With no further attempt at escape Mahendra and the Mahatma followed the sepoys. As they were being taken along the street, Mahatma Satya said to the lieutenant:

"Gentle sir, I am very fond of singing devotional songs. Do you have any objection to my singing such songs?"

"No, you may sing your hymns," said the lieutenant who rather liked the Mahatma. "I have no objection. You are a true *sanyasi*, and I feel that you will be acquitted. But this rogue here will be hanged on the gallows."

So, in Sanskrit which his captors could not understand, Mahatma Satya sang:

"Fanned by gentle breezes
There lies a woman on the bank of a river
That gentle lady is much afflicted,
O, my hero, please do not neglect
To rush thither to her aid right away.
And Sukumari runs wild there by that river."

Upon their arrival in the city, both Mahendra and the Mahatma were taken straight to the Chief of Police. That official reported the case to the government, and locked up the prisoners in the city jail, a frightful place from which few prisoners ever came out alive.

Chapter 14

It was night. The two prisoners were together in a cell.

"Mahendra," the Mahatma said, "this is a joyous occasion. Tonight we are in jail. Now say *Bande Mataram.*"

In a tone of indifference Mahendra repeated the words.

"What makes you so sad, my child?" Mahatma Satya asked. "If you had taken the vow of renunciation you would have had to give up your wife and child anyway. You could have kept no connection with them whatsoever."

"Renunciation is quite a different thing from separation by death," Mahendra retorted gravely. "The power that inspired me to think of the new life disappeared with the death of my wife and child."

"You will regain that power within yourself. I shall give you the required strength of mind. Accept the initiation, and take the vow now."

"My wife and child are being devoured by the beasts of the jungle! Do not talk of your initiation to me now," Mahendra said in a voice that showed his unwillingness to talk of such things at the moment.

"Please do not worry about that. The Children have cremated your wife's dead body, and they have placed your child with a proper family."

Surprised to hear this, Mahendra refused to believe it.

"How do you know that?" he asked. "You have been with me all this time."

"We are the initiates of a great cause. God is ever kind to us. You will receive news tonight. And tonight you will be free from this dungeon."

When Mahendra said not a word, the Mahatma realized that his fellow-prisoner refused to believe him.

"I know you do not believe my words, Mahendra," Mahatma Satya said. "But why not test them out before you make up your mind about them." He thereupon walked to the gate of the prison.

Mahendra could not see what his companion was doing in the dark, but he sensed that he was talking with some one there. When the Mahatma returned, Mahendra asked him, "What test?"

"You are about to win your freedom from this jail."

At that moment the door of the cell opened. A guard entered the cell and asked:

"Whose name is Mahendra Singh?"

"My name is Mahendra Singh," Mahendra said.

"We have orders for your release; you may go," the guard informed him.

Mahendra was at first astonished, for he thought it was a trick. But as a test, he walked out of the cell. No one stopped him, and he walked straight to the public street.

Taking advantage of Mahendra's departure, the guard said to the Mahatma:

"Master, why don't you, too, walk out? I have come for you."

"Who are you? Are you Dhiren?" the Mahatma asked.

"Yes, Master, I am Dhiren."

"How is it you are a guard here?"

"Bhavan sent me. Upon my arrival in the city I learned that you were locked up in this jail. So I secured some hemp mixed with *dhutra*. The guard smoked the hemp, and is now sleeping. This uniform, this turban, this spear, in fact all that I have on, belong to him."

"You may get out of the city in that uniform. I cannot free myself this way."

"Why, what has happened, Master?"

"Today is the day of a supreme test for the Children!"

And just then Mahendra returned.

"What made you come back here, Mahendra?" the Mahatma asked.

"You are certainly a Master. And I simply cannot leave you here alone."

"Then stay here with me. We both will win our freedom tonight in a different way."

Mahendra Singh was happy beyond words. Dhiren went away. Mahendra and the Mahatma remained within the prison.

Chapter 15

In the forest a number of the Children had heard the song Mahatma Satya sang. But Jiban, above all, understood its real message. He had had, in the very beginning, the Mahatma's command to follow the movements of Mahendra. In this assignment he had met on the roadside a woman who had had no food for seven days. Jiban revived her with food and drink, but at parting swore at her for having caused him delay. Then he saw his master being taken away by the sepoys and heard him sing the song. Jiban well understood all the code signals of the Mahatma.

He interpreted the song and the melody as a command to rush to the aid of a woman lying helpless by the river. Jiban had seen his master in the hands of the British, and he felt that his first duty was to release the Mahatma by any means. But he thought within himself: "This is not the meaning of the master's message. To obey his orders is much more important than to save his life. This was the first lesson I learnt from him."

So he walked slowly along the river. At a little distance under a tree he discovered a dead woman and her living child. He had never seen Mahendra's wife and child, but he had seen Mahendra with the Mahatma. Consequently he reasoned: "The woman may be Mahendra's wife, and the girl his daughter. Whoever they may be, the mother is dead; and the daughter is still alive. The first thing to do is to save the life of the child, otherwise she will be eaten up by the tigers and the bears of the jungle. Bhavan is somewhere around. He will attend to the cremation of this woman." He picked up the child and walked away.

With the child in his arms, Jiban entered the thick forest. Beyond the jungle he came to a village by the name of Bharuipur, where a few families of simple country folk lived. Beyond it again there lay another vast forest—and forests on all sides, so that the village was like an island surrounded by an ocean of forests.

Bharuipur was small, but very beautiful. There were velvety pastures and delightful groves of mango, jack, plum and palm trees, their branches and leaves green and soft. In a lake of blue water played cranes, ducks, and gallinules. On the banks around the lake cuckoos and geese abounded. At a little distance peacocks were dancing. Every family in the village had cows in the yard. But the granaries were empty, and on all sides signs of destitution were to be seen. From the ceiling of one house hung a myna cage. A few houses had sacramental paintings on their walls; and a few families had vegetable gardens in their yards. All had been equally affected by the famine. Men, women and children were weak, emaciated and miserable. And, yet, the people of this village had no idea of the worst of the famine. The jungles yielded various kinds of food fit for humans to eat. This fact helped to protect the villagers from the dangers of sickness and saved their lives.

A little home was standing in the midst of an extensive mango grove. A mud wall surrounded the homestead. On each of the four sides of a courtyard a house stood. They had cows, goats, a peacock, even a chattering myna bird. They had had a monkey, but it was so difficult to feed that they had to let it go. In the barn there was a rice husker, and a lemon tree in the yard. There were also a few jasmine plants but none of them had borne flowers this year. On every verandah of the houses there was a spinning wheel.

Few people were around when Jiban entered the yard with the child in his arms. He walked up to the verandah of one of the houses and started a spinning wheel on its whining way. The child had never heard the noise of a *charka* before. She had been crying a little ever since she had been separated from her mother. Now, frightened by the strange noise, she screamed at the top of her voice. At the child's cry a young lady of seventeen or eighteen rushed out of the house. She was amazed at what she saw. As she stood, her head bent and forefinger on her cheek, she spoke:

"Brother Jiban, what is this? What makes you spin the wheel? Where did you get the child? Is this your child? Pehaps you have married again?"

As Jiban handed the child to his sister, he shook her in affectionate reproach and said:

"My naughty sister, how can I have a child? Do you think I am so worthless? Have you any milk in the house?"

"Certainly, we have milk," she replied, and then hurried into the house to warm some while Jiban played with the spinning wheel on the verandah.

Sukumari had stopped crying the moment she was taken into the young lady's arms. Perhaps the little girl accepted her hostess as her own mother, for the lady was pretty, like a lotus blossom. Within the house the child cried but once, perhaps with the warmth from the heat of the stove. Jiban, hearing this cry, called out:

"O, Nimi, my little sister, haven't you finished warming the milk yet?"

"Yes, brother," Nimi replied, as she brought a big cup of milk.

Nimi sat on the floor, placed the child flat on her lap, and began feeding her with a spoon. Suddenly tears fell from her beautiful eyes. The spoon had belonged to a child of her own that had died. Wiping the tears from her eyes, Nimi smiled and asked: "Tell me, brother, whose daughter is she?"

"What makes you so interested in knowing that, my naughty little sister?"

"Will you give me the girl?"

"What will you do with her?"

"I shall feed her, fondle her in my arms, and nurse her as my very own."

Again tears filled her eyes; and again she wiped them away and smiled.

"You will have no use for her," Jiban said. "You will have children of your own."

"That may be. But please let me have this child now. You may take her away afterwards."

"All right, you may have her. Once in a while I shall come down to see her. She belongs to the *Kshatrya* caste. Now I must go."

"But you must eat something before you go, brother. It is already late for luncheon. I beg of you, please eat something before you go."

"Well, if you insist, I shall take a little rice and curry."

Within a few minutes Nimi had the dinner served for her brother. Jiban had before him milk-white rice, *Kalai* pea soup, wild figs, curried carp caught from the pond, and milk.

"Nimi, my dear sister," Jiban remarked. "Who says that we are going through a famine? Perhaps famine has not touched your village yet! Is it so?"

"Famine has reached here all right. This famine is frightful indeed! But we are only two in the family. Whatever we have we share with others and thus get along. We had rain in our village. Don't you remember? You said it would rain; so it did. Thus in our village the rice crop did not altogether fail. Others sold their rice in the city—but we did not."

"Where is my brother-in-law, Nimi?"

"A neighboring family needs food." Nimi whispered as she looked at the floor. "So he has gone out with a few pounds of rice."

Jiban had not eaten such a sumptuous meal in many a moon. Without wasting words he quickly finished the repast. Nimi had cooked only enough for herself and her husband, and had given her own share to her brother. When she found his plate empty, she also gave him her husband's share, and in a few minutes Jiban finished that too.

"May I serve you anything more, brother?" Nimi asked.

"What else have you?"

"I have a ripe jack-fruit."

"Excellent."

And Nimi served the jack-fruit, which Jiban ate without a word of protest.

"Brother, that's all. I have nothing more to offer you," Nimi said, laughing.

"Well, then I shall return some other time and once more eat dishes like these."

Nimi was at last forced to offer him water for washing.

"Brother, I have a request for you," Nimi said as she poured water into his hands.

"What is it, Nimi?"

"Do you promise that you will grant me the favor?"

"First tell me what it is."

"But you won't disappoint me, will you?"

"What is it, my dear little sister?"

Then she pressed the fingers of her left hand with

those of her right; looked at her fingers; then looked at Jiban, and again on the floor. At last she summoned courage enough to say:

"May I bring my *bowdi* here?"

"Give my child back to me," Jiban said, furious at such a request. "And on another such occasion I shall return the food you fed me with. You wicked girl, you always say the things you should never mention to me."

"I may be bad and naughty and all that; but may I fetch your wife here for a moment, that she may see you just once before you return to the *Ashram* of the Mother?"

"I must go now. I must go." And Jiban started quickly from the room. But Nimi rushed to the door, closed it, stood against it and said:

"You must kill me before you can go. You will see your wife before you leave this house."

"Do you realize how many enemies of our Motherland I have killed so far?"

"Bravo! Bravo! What a thing to be proud of!" Nimi said angrily. "You renounce your wife. You kill human beings. And then you want me to be afraid of you! But I tell you that we are children of the same father. If you have come to such a state that you are proud of killing human beings, then kill me, and you will have a chance to brag of having killed your own sister. Shame on you, to kill human beings and then boast of it!"

"Well, then go and get your *bowdi*," Jiban said as he laughed. "This time I forgive you, but if you ever again even suggest such a thing, I may or may not punish you; but be sure that by way of an insult I shall shave the head of your husband, bathe it in buttermilk and then place him on the hind end of a donkey, and run him out of the village."

"Oh, what a relief that would be." Nimi smiled as she hurried from the room. She ran to a humble cottage near by. Inside the cottage sat a woman in rags. The woman's hair was untidy. She was spinning.

"Hurry, sister, hurry," Nimi said.

"Why, what has happened, sister? Has your husband beaten you? Must I apply healing oil to the wounds?"

"Pretty near, sister, pretty near. Have you any oil here?"

The sister-in-law handed Nimi a cup containing oil. Nimi immediately began to dress her sister-in-law's hair with it. Then she affectionately patted the woman on the cheeks and said: "You are dressed in rags now. Where is that beautiful Dacca *sari* of yours?"

"Have you gone crazy, sister?"

"There is no time to lose. Please get your *sari* out quickly."

In fun the sister-in-law got her *sari*. Even the dire sorrow of her life had failed to crush the joy of her soul. She was young. The freshness of her youth was like the glory of a fullblown blossom. She lived in sackcloth and ashes, and fasting had become her only food. Yet her radiant beauty blossomed through the humble rags that covered her body. As dwells lightning in the clouds, brilliance in the mind, music in words, happiness in death, so there dwelt in her beauty an intangible glory. Yes, peerless devotion adorned her divinely. Smilingly she took her Dacca *sari* from its hiding place, handed it to Nimi and said:

"Here you are. Here is the Dacca *sari*. What are you going to do with it?"

"You have to wear it today," Nimi said.

"Why should I put that *sari* on?"

"My brother is home. He wants to see you," Nimi whispered, placing her beautiful arms around the graceful neck of her sister-in-law.

"If he wants to see me, then there is no reason why I should put on my beautiful *sari*. Let me go as I am, in these rags."

And the sister-in-law threw the *sari* aside; she placed her arm around Nimi's neck and then walked out of the cottage. Nimi accompanied her to the door of her own house, made her enter, closed the door, and she herself remained outside.

Chapter 16

THE young woman who entered the house was about twenty-five years old, and yet she looked no older than Nimi. As she crossed the threshold in her dull and torn *sari*, the house became lighted with the lustre of her beauty, as if hundreds of buds that had lain hidden behind leaves suddenly blossomed; as if some one had broken open a sealed jar of rare perfume or had thrown a perfumed incense into a dying fire. In vain the beautiful lady searched the house for her husband. He was nowhere to be found. At last she went out of the house and found him in the yard leaning against the trunk of a mango tree. He was weeping as if his heart would break.

The woman approached him gently, and quietly placed his hands in her own. It would be idle to deny that she felt like crying. Providence only knew that the stream of tears that gathered in her eyes was sufficient to drown Jiban in its torrents. Yet she restrained her tears and said: "Please do not weep. I know you are sorry for me. I am happy indeed in whatever state of existence you have placed me. Please do not cry for me."

"Shanti, why do I see you dressed in rags?" Jiban asked as he lifted his face and wiped his tears. "You should not be in need of anything in the world."

"I have kept your wealth intact for you," Shanti replied. "I have no use for money. But will you accept me as your wife when you return home?"

"Why do you ask such a question, Shanti? I have not deserted you, my best beloved!"

"I do not mean desertion. But will you love me as before when you return home from the fulfillment of your vow?"

Before she could finish, Jiban embraced her fervently. With his head on her shoulder, he said: "I am sorry, sorry indeed that I wanted to see you now."

"You have thus broken your vow?" Shanti asked anxiously.

"I am not afraid of that, Shanti! There is atonement for broken vows. It is only that it will be difficult for me to return to the *Ashram* of the Mother after having looked at your face again. That's why I told Nimi that I did not want to see you. I knew that I could not return to my national duty if I looked at your divine face, Shanti, dearest. Place religion, money, ambition, salvation, society, vows, devotional rites, rituals, prayers, sacraments and all that is involved on this earth—yes, place all these on one side of the scale, and you, and you alone on the other; and I swear by the holy name of

Mother India herself that I do not know which side weighs heavier, my dearest Shanti!

"India is quiet. She is almost dead. What can I do with the country? If I get but an acre of land somewhere I can create a heaven if only I have you there. What shall I do with the country? The sorrows of my countrymen? Yes, sorrows indeed! But is there a more sorrowful figure in the country than the man who is fortunate enough to obtain, and then renounces, a wife like you? Who in this country is poorer than the man who has just seen you in rags?

"You are my helpmate in all the noble deeds of my life. Yet with a rifle in my hands I roam alone in the hills, on the plains and in the forests, killing the enemies of our country's freedom. I do not know whether the country will be ours again or not. But this I do know, that you are mine and I am yours. You are greater than this country. You are my heaven itself. Come, let us go home. I shall not return to the *Ashram* again."

For a while Shanti could not utter a word. She thought intently, and said: "Shame on you! You are a hero! The greatest happiness in my life is that I am the wife of a hero. And you want to renounce the path of heroism just for the sake of a wife? Do not love me so. I am willing to deprive myself even of that happiness, but never forsake your path of duty. Now tell me, what is the price for this violation of your vow?"

"Atonement—Oh, that is very simple. It is by fasting a little; and also by giving alms of only a few coins. That's very simple, Shanti, very simple!"

"I happen to know the nature of the atonement for such sins!" she retorted, smiling. "But I wonder if the punishment for a single offense is the same as for a hundred such offenses?"

"Why do you ask such questions?" Jiban inquired in sorrow and in surprise.

"I have only one request to make of you. Please do not make atonement for this breach of vow before you meet me again."

"You may rest assured of that, Shanti. I am not going to die before seeing you again; that is certain. There is no hurry for death anyway. I must not stay here any longer. But my eyes are still hungry, and my soul thirsty to see you. Some day we are sure to meet each other when time will not count. And some day we shall reach the destined land of our heart's desire. I must go now. But, please honor a request of mine. Please give up this dress of yours; and go to live in my ancestral mansion."

"Where are you going now?"

"I must return to the *Ashram* and search for the Mahatma. I am worried about the manner in which he went to the city. If I don't obtain any news of him at the *Ashram*, then I myself must hurry to the city without the least delay.

Chapter 17

At the *Ashram* of the Mother, Bhavan was engaged in singing devotional songs. Suddenly there stood in front of him a spirited Child by the name of Jnan.

"Why do you look so grave?" Bhavan asked.

"It seems that trouble is in the air," Jnan said. "The British have gone almost insane over that episode of yesterday. They are arresting yellow-robed men at sight. All our comrades have given up yellow robes today. Mahatma Satya alone went towards the city dressed in yellow. That will be the end of him."

"The Englishman is not born who can keep Mahatma Satya a captive! I know that Dhiren has followed him. And yet I must go to the city too. You remain to protect the *Ashram*."

Bhavan immediately entered a secret chamber and selected some clothes. In a short time he was transformed. Instead of the yellow robe of the order, he had dressed himself in a pleated pajama, a *mirjai* and *kaba*.

He put on slippers and a turban. He removed from his face the marks of sandal paste and added a jet black beard and moustache. He looked exactly like a young Moghul nobleman. Thus dressed and fully armed, he stepped out of the *Ashram*.

About two miles from the *Ashram*, there were two points on a hill, peaks covered with thick forests. Between these two peaks there was a secret depot. Numerous horses were raised there. It was the military stable of the Children. Bhavan caught a horse, saddled it and galloped towards the city.

On the way he was stopped by a strange sight. Like a fallen star from the blue above, or like a streak of lightning from its home in the clouds, there lay on the banks of the singing river the body of a radiantly beautiful woman. There was no sign of life in her, and an empty box of poison lay beside her. Bhavan was surprised, angry and afraid. Like Jiban, he had never seen Mahendra's wife and child. But in Bhavan's case the circumstances that had led Jiban to take them for the wife and child of Mahendra were absent. He had not seen Mahatma Satya and Mahendra being led prisoners by the sepoys. Besides the child was no longer there. From the little box he inferred that the woman had taken poison in order to commit suicide. He alighted from his horse. Sitting by the dead body, he debated within himself for a long time. He examined her forehead, hands and sides. This holyman knew many mysterious secrets of life, death and healing. "There is still time," he thought, "to revive her. A spark of life still lingers in her body. But what is the use of restoring life to her?"

At first he did not know what to do. He thought and thought, and pondered a thousand and one things. Finally he entered the forest and plucked leaves from a certain tree. He crushed some of these leaves between his hands for juice. Then he forcibly parted the woman's lips and jaws, and with the aid of his fingers, forced some of the juice into her mouth. He applied some of the same juice inside her nostrils. Then he massaged her body with it. He repeated this process over and over again.

Now and then he placed his hand to her nostrils to find if breathing had started anew. For a while it seemed that his efforts were fruitless but he persevered in the experiment. At last his face brightened, as he felt a faint breath on his fingers. He applied more of the juice. Slowly her breathing gained strength. Her pulsation started. Kalyani began to open her eyes slowly, very slowly. It was like the deepening of the faint rays of the sun at dawn; it was like the gentle opening of the lotus buds in the morning; and it was like the first dawning of love in a human heart. Bhavan placed the half-conscious woman on the back of his horse, and rapidly bore her away to the city.

Chapter 18

BEFORE dusk the Children came to know that both Mahatma Satya and Mahendra were prisoners in jail in the city. Slowly they gathered in hundreds, until they filled the forests around the *Ashram* of Mother India. The fire of anger was in their eyes, and the passion of stern determination on their lips; and one could hear proud words of revenge from their mouths. Soon thousands of Children had assembled. At the gate of the main building, Jiban appeared, sword in hand, and thus spoke aloud:

"For a long time we have been thinking of destroying, root and branch, British rule in India, and then of drowning it in the depths of the seas, and thus of purifying Mother India from the pollution of this alien domination. Brothers, that day is here today! Our leader, Mahatma Satya is of infinite wisdom. He is pure. He is a humanitarian. He is a patriot. We all follow his leadership. We all love him. And today he lies prisoner in a British jail! Have our swords grown rusty? Have we no strength left in our arms? Have we no courage in our hearts? Brothers, sing *Bande Mataram—Bande Mataram —Bande Mataram*.

"Let us now get together to crush British rule in India under our feet. Let us burn their sceptre into ashes, and then scatter the ashes to the winds. Brothers, sing *Bande Mataram* again!"

Instantly the entire forest shook with the chant of *Bande Mataram*. Thousands of swords cried out for the enemy's blood. Thousands of spears lifted their defiant heads to the skies. The noise of the arms was as the roar of thunder. The drums struck the *Bande Mataram*. The noise grew so intense that many a bird and animal left the jungle. The birds covered the skies with their wings, and filled the air with their cries of fear. Again hundreds of drums began to roar. Then the Children, chanting the *Bande Mataram*, emerged from the woods in files. In the darkness of the night they began to march towards the city in firm, dignified step.

They reached the city only to disrupt it. At the sudden and unexpected attack the citizens became panic-stricken and ran in all directions. The police lost their wits and were paralyzed with terror.

First of all, the Children attacked the city jail, killing the guards and triumphantly freeing the Mahatma and Mahendra. They carried the two released men on their shoulders in a delirium of happiness dancing and shouting *Bande Mataram* to shake the city to its very foundations. Then they attacked and burnt the homes of Englishmen wherever they found them. But

Mahatma Satya commanded that there should be no unnecessary destruction of life and property.

The British were aghast at this attack on the city, and at once dispatched a contingent of provincial sepoys to suppress the rebels. In addition to rifles, the sepoys had a cannon with them. At the news of their advance, the Children again emerged ready for battle from the jungles around the *Ashram* of Mother India. But how could their *lathis*, spears and rifles cope with British cannon? The Children were defeated.

Book 2

Chapter 1

SHANTI had lost her mother in infancy. This had played its part in the formation of her character. Her father had been a Brahmin, professor in his own Sanskrit Academy. As he had no other female in the family, Shanti was wont to attend her father's classes. A few students lived at the academy and little Shanti used to visit them at times to play with them, and they grew to be very fond of her.

The first fruit of Shanti's association with students alone was that she failed to learn how to dress like a girl; or if she did, she gave it up and dressed herself like a boy. If perchance any one ever dressed her as a girl, she herself changed the *sari* into a *dhoti* and garbed herself like a boy again. As she never dressed her hair like a girl's, the students were fond of combing it into curls with a wooden comb; and the curls fell on her back, on her shoulders, on her arms, and on her cheeks. Like the students, she was in the habit of putting holy marks on her forehead, and sandal paste on her body.

And she cried bitterly indeed when she was forbidden to use the sacred thread meant only for male Brahmins. At the time of prayer and meditation, she never forgot to imitate the students of the academy. In the absence of the professor, the students at times entertained themselves with stories and doubtful jokes in Sanskrit. Like a parrot Shanti memorized those tales, of course without knowing what they meant.

As Shanti grew up she began to learn what the students were studying. She did not know anything about Sanskrit grammar; but she memorized verses from *Bhatti Kabyam*, *Raghubangsam*, *Kumarsambhavam*, *Naishadhacharitam* and other Sanskrit works of importance. Her father, noticing the literary tendencies of his motherless daughter, at last began to teach her the *Mughdhobodha* Sanskrit grammar. Shanti learned the grammar so quickly that her father was surprised indeed, and taught her a few books of Sanskrit literature.

Then, quite unexpectedly, the professor died. The academy closed. Shanti became a homeless orphan. The students left. But they all loved Shanti and could not leave her helpless. One of them took her to his own home. This young student later joined the Order of the Children, and became known as Jiban. Jiban's parents were alive. He introduced Shanti to them.

"Who will take the responsibility for someone else's daughter?" Jiban's father asked.

"I have brought her here, and I will undertake the full responsibility of Shanti," Jiban replied.

The parents, however, as Jiban was a bachelor, and

Shanti approaching womanhood, proposed a match between the two. Without more ado Shanti was married to Jiban.

After the marriage the parents came to realize that they had done the wrong thing—that the marriage perhaps had been a mistake, for Shanti stubbornly refused to dress as a girl, and would not even fix her hair like a girl's. She was scarcely ever at home, but would mingle with the boys of the neighborhood and play with them like a tomboy. She used to enter the neighboring jungles alone and search for peacocks, deer, and rare fruits and flowers. Her parents-in-law at first simply asked her not to do such things. Then they rebuked her. Punishment followed rebuke; and finally they were forced to confine Shanti to the house. At these tyrannies Shanti felt much afflicted. So once at an opportune moment she left home without telling even Jiban of her plans.

She entered the jungle, and selecting proper flowers for her purpose, dyed her dress yellow, at once transforming herself into a young *sanyasi*. In those days multitudes of *sanyasis* roamed about Bengal. Shanti lived on alms, and at last stood on the road to the holy shrine of Jagganath at Puri. Within a short time there appeared a group of *sanyasis*. Shanti joined them.

The *sanyasis* of those days were of a different type from those of today. They were united, well educated, strong; and knew the science of warfare. And they were endowed with other qualities too. Generally they were rebels against the British occupation of India. They lost no opportunity in capturing the properties of the alien government. They never failed to gather strong children every chance they got. These they educated and trained in the use of arms, and thus added to the strength of their own community.

It was with one such community of *sanyasis*, that Shanti found herself. Noticing the slender body of Shanti, they at first hesitated to accept her; but when they came to know her cleverness, the high culture of her mind and her ability for work, they accepted her with open arms. In this community Shanti learned gymnastics and the use of arms, and soon became strong and hardy. She traveled with them far and near, taking part in many a fray, and became expert in the use of the weapons of war.

Gradually, however, she manifested signs of her sex. Many of the *sanyasis* came to know that young Shanti was a woman in disguise. But *sanyasis* in general were above sex, and they did not object to the continuance of her association. There were many scholars among them and one of them undertook to teach Shanti. I said that the *sanyasis* were generally above the demands of sex, but this *pandit* was not. Or it may be that the youth and ravishing beauty of Shanti were responsible for his lack of restraint. His senses arose to torture him again. He began to teach Shanti poems of romance with strong amorous appeal, and he was wont to explain these sensuous poems to her with vulgar frankness.

Instead of hurting Shanti, this helped her. She had never known what bashfulness was. Now feminine modesty slowly entered her heart. As the radiance of feminine grace began to rise above her acquired masculine habits, the rare qualities of her personality shone beautifully. She gave up her studies with this teacher.

But as a hunter follows the doe, so this teacher followed Shanti. She, however, had acquired, through gymnastic exercises, a strength of which few men could boast. Whenever he came near her, she fought him. Once this sensuous man found her alone, and caught her tightly by her left hand. She could not free herself; but with her right fist she struck such a blow on the *pandit's* forehead that he fell unconscious to the ground. Then she left this group of *sanyasis*.

Shanti was fearless. Alone she started for home. Her courage and strength protected her all the way. She lived by alms or on wild fruits. She fought many fights alone, and always won. Eventually she reached home, but her father-in-law closed his doors against her. He did not want to lose caste in the community. Shanti had left home, and certainly could not be taken back now into the family. So she went away without a word of protest. But Jiban was at home; he followed her and soon overtook her.

"Why did you leave home, Shanti?" Jiban asked. "Where have you been all this time?"

Shanti told him nothing but the truth. And Jiban who could tell the difference between truth and falsehood, believed every word she uttered.

Cupid never wastes his darts, so carefully made from the lustre of the amorous glances of the most charming damsels in heaven. And he does not by any means waste such darts on the married. Cupid never wastes his time doing useless things, unlike human beings who always seem to enjoy doing the unnecessary; and not only human beings, for at times even the moon can be seen in the skies after the rising of the sun. Lord *Indra* showers rain on the ocean. *Kuber*, Lord of wealth, always likes to fill chests that are already overflowing with wealth. *Yama*, Lord of death, enjoys taking away the only surviving member of a family when others are gone. But Cupid never wastes his darts on the married. He leaves married couples in the hands of *Projapati*, and studiously goes after those with whose heartblood he can easily play. But today, perhaps Cupid had nothing else to do, perhaps he was enjoying a holiday. So he nonchalantly shot two of his darts. One went right through the heart of Jiban. And the other fell on Shanti's heart to tell her that her heart was, after all, the heart of a woman—a tender heart, yes, very, very tender indeed!

Suddenly the bud of her heart opened its petals into a full-blown blossom of love. And with deep and smiling eyes she looked at Jiban's face.

"I will not disown you," Jiban said. "Please stay here until I return."

"Are you sure to return?" Shanti inquired.

Jiban could not wait to reply nor did he even look to see if anybody were near. In the shade of the cocoanut trees he pressed his lips gently against Shanti's and ran off, feeling as if he had drunk the nectar that can be found only in heaven. He returned home in a rush, explained everything, and said goodbye to his mother.

Recently his sister, Nimi, had married a gentleman of Bharuipur. He was very fond of this brother-in-law. So Jiban took his wife to Bharuipur. His brother-in-law gave him a plot of land; and Jiban built a little cottage on it. Both Shanti and Jiban passed their days there in unalloyed happiness. Thus living with her husband, Shanti's tomboy qualities gradually began to disappear. The feminine within her began daily to unfold itself. The two passed their days and nights as in a dream. But suddenly this dream came to an end. Jiban met Mahatma Satya, left his wife and joined the Order of the Children. For the first time since this separation they met at the meeting arranged by Nimi.

Chapter 2

AFTER Jiban's departure, Shanti sat on the verandah of Nimi's house. Nimi came out and, with the child in her lap, sat near Shanti. There was not even the least trace of tears in Shanti's eyes. She looked cheerful. Now and then she smiled a little, and then she was grave and pensive; but her thoughts were elsewhere. Nimi understood Shanti's mood.

"Isn't it nice, Shanti, that you met my brother?" Nimi asked. Shanti said nothing. Nimi felt that her sister was not in a mood to give expression to her thoughts. She knew too that Shanti was never fond of speaking her inner thoughts. So she changed the topic of conversation by asking: "Look here, sister, how do you like my child?"

"Where did you get the child, sister?" Shanti asked. "When did you give birth to a baby?"

"Good gracious! You should be ashamed of yourself. The child is not mine. She is my brother's child."

Nothing was further from Nimi's thoughts than to

hurt the feelings of her brother's wife. She merely meant that she had obtained the child from her brother.

Shanti, however, did not take it so generously. She thought that perhaps her sister meant to hurt her feelings by this taunt.

"I did not ask you about the father of the child, but of her mother, sister!"

Nimi was rightly served. She felt embarrassed.

"Dear sister," Nimi said gravely, "how can I tell you whose daughter she is? I forgot to ask brother about her in my hurry. Perhaps brother picked her up somewhere. In these famine days even mothers are deserting their children. You know how so many parents come to us to sell their children. But who cares to nurture other people's children?"

Again her eyes became moistened with tears. She wiped them away and said:

"Oh, such a beautiful girl! She is as beautiful as the moon; and so plump—I begged brother to give me the child, and he did."

For a long time they talked on various subjects. In the meantime Nimi's husband returned and Shanti walked back to her own cottage and locked herself in. Then she picked up and saved a portion of the ashes in the oven. As she stood on the floor, she thought for a long time. At last she spoke thus to herself:

"Tonight I am actually going to do what I have been thinking of doing for a long time. The hope that kept me from doing it has met with success. Well, is it a success, or is it a failure? This life of mine itself is a failure! I must carry out my resolution. The punishment is the same for one or a hundred breaches of a solemn vow."

Then she threw away the rice and curry she had cooked for her dinner. Plucking a few fruits from the garden, she ate those instead. Next she picked up her beautiful Dacca *sari;* and tearing away the borders, she dyed the cloth yellow. It was almost dusk when she had finished dyeing and drying the borderless piece of cloth. Closing the door of her cottage, she engaged herself in another task. She scissored off a part of her long and shaggy hair and saved it carefully; then braided whatever was left on her head. Her head thus became covered with the *jatas* of a *sanyasi.* She cut the yellow cloth in two, put one part on, and tied the other around her breast.

There was a little mirror in the cottage. For a long time Shanti looked at her dress in this mirror.

"I really do not know," Shanti said to herself, "what to do to finish this task."

She threw away the mirror. With the hair she had cut off, she made a beard and moustache. She did not put on this artificial beard and moustache then, but saved them to fool someone at the proper time. Then she picked up a large deerskin, and covered herself with it from her neck to her knees. Thus dressed, the young *sanyasi* looked around the cottage to be sure that she was alone there. Exactly at midnight she opened the door and entered the deep forests alone in the guise of a holyman. That night the wood nymphs heard this wonderful song sung divinely:

"Maiden, where dost thou go,
Thus trotting on horseback?"
"To battle I go, please stand not in my way,
Please stand not in my way.
So I sing *Bande Mataram, Bande Mataram, Bande Mataram.*
And today I plunge right into the waves of warfare;
Who art thou and who is thine and why dost thou follow me?

"Oh woman, who cares to be a woman today?
Our fight is on—our fight is on!
So sing victory to Mother India,
Victory, victory to Mother India.
I beg of you, my beloved, please
Do not leave me behind.
Leave me not, leave me not.
Hark, hark, there beat the drums of victory!
And look! my war-horse neighs and paws
To go to war, yes, to go to war to free India
From England's yoke.
I cannot—I cannot stay at home any longer.
Oh, woman! Who cares to be a woman today?
Our fight is on—our fight is on!
So sing victory, victory to Mother India,
Victory, victory to Mother India—
Bande Mataram! Bande Mataram! Bande Mataram!"

Chapter 3

NEXT day the three discouraged leaders of the Children were seated in one of the secluded rooms of the *Ashram*. They were engaged in conversation.

"Master Satya, why is God so unfavorable to us?" Jiban asked. "For what sin of ours were we thus defeated by the British?"

"God is not unfavorable to us," Mahatma Satya replied. "Warfare is composed of both victory and defeat. The other day we were victorious. Yesterday we met with defeat. He who wins last really wins. I am fully confident that God will again smile on our efforts. He has ever been kind to us. In His name we must reach the goal of our mission. We shall indeed suffer the tortures of hell if we meet with defeat in the end; but I am sure of our success. We must remember, however, that as we can never win victory without the grace of God, even so we must use our own utmost efforts too. The chief cause of our defeat is that we are without proper arms and ammunition. How can *lathis* and spears withstand the onslaught of cannon and rifles? Now our duty is to see that we are fully and plentifully equipped with modern weapons."

"That is a most difficult task, Master," Jiban said.

"Most difficult, Jiban! You—a Child, utter such words? There is no such word as 'difficult' for a Child."

"How can we obtain modern arms and ammunition? Master, please command!"

"To-night I am going on a pilgrimage to gather arms and ammunition for our victory. Undertake no serious work until I return, but by all means preserve the unity of the Children. Provide for their sustenance and fill our treasuries with money for the Mother's victory. I entrust you two with this work."

"Master," Bhavan said, "how can you gather arms by going on a pilgrimage? You cannot purchase cannon and rifles and munitions, and ship them here. Where can you find the quantities we need to fight the British. Who is going to sell them? And who is going to carry them here?"

"We cannot, of course, purchase enough to meet our needs. I shall send experts to manufacture them here."

"Do you mean here, at this *Ashram?*" Jiban inquired.

"No, that is impossible! For a long time I have been thinking of these problems. God has opened a way for us today. You say God is against us; but I find God is very kind to us."

"Where can we establish a factory?" Bhavan asked.

"At Padachina," Mahatma Satya said gravely.

"What do you mean? How can we do that there?" Jiban asked.

"Why do you think I have been entreating Mahendra Singh to take the vow?" said the Mahatma.

"Has Mahendra taken the vow?"

"Not yet; but he will. I am going to initiate him tonight."

"We do not know," Jiban said, "what efforts have been made for the initiation of Mahendra nor do we know what happened to his wife and child; neither do we know where they are. Today I found a little girl by the river and have left her with my sister. A beautiful woman lay dead by the child. I wonder if these were Mahendra's wife and child?"

"Yes, they were Mahendra's wife and child."

Bhavan was startled to hear this and at once realized that the woman he had revived was Mahendra's wife. But he did not think it necessary to say anything just yet.

"How did Mahendra's wife die?" Jiban asked.

"She took poison," Mahatma Satya said.

"Why did she take poison?"

"In a dream she was commanded to die."

"Was that meant for the fulfillment of our mission?"

"Mahendra thinks so. It is about dusk. I must now attend to my evening prayer and meditation. Then I shall initiate the new Children," the Mahatma said.

"Why do you say Children? Does anyone else beside Mahendra aspire to be your personal disciple?" Bhavan asked in a tone of surprise.

"Yes, there is a new Child. I never saw him before. He came to me today for the first time. He is very young but I am highly pleased with his looks, manner and intelligence. He appears to be real gold. I shall entrust Jiban with the task of training him as a Child. Jiban is clever in attracting human hearts! I must go now. But I have special advice for you. Please listen to me most carefully."

Both Bhavan and Jiban joined palms in salutation, bowed their heads in reverence, and said:

"Please command us."

"If either of you has already done anything wrong or does anything wrong in my absence, make no atonement until I return from my pilgrimage. You shall have to make atonement upon my return."

With these words Mahatma Satya retired to his own quarters. Bhavan and Jiban continued to look at each other strangely. At last Bhavan said to Jiban:

"Is that meant for you?"

"Perhaps," Jiban replied. "I went home to leave Mahendra's child with my sister."

"There is no harm in that. That is not forbidden. But—did you meet your wife?"

"Perhaps that is what the Master suspects."

Chapter 4

PRAYER and meditation over, Mahatma Satya called Mahendra and said to him:

"Mahendra, your daughter is alive."

"Where is she, Master?" Mahendra asked anxiously.

"Before you know that, tell me the truth. Are you willing to join the Order of the Children?"

"Most decidedly."

"Then, please do not ask the whereabouts of your daughter."

"Why, Master?"

"He who joins this order can keep no connection whatsoever with his wife, son, daughter or any other relative. There is properly prescribed atonement if even he look at the faces of his wife and children. Until the Children win victory, you may not see the face of your daughter. If you have really decided to join the Children, then why know her whereabouts? You may not see her."

"Why such cruel laws? Mahatma?"

"The duty of the Children is hard. He alone is worthy of this duty who has renounced everything for the sake of Mother India. The man whose heart is tied with the strings of human attachment is like a kite that is tied to the reel; it cannot fly high or far from the earth below."

"Master, perhaps I do not fully understand you. Do you mean to say that the man who sees his wife and children is not fit for serious work?"

"We forget our higher duties the moment we look at our wives and children. A Child of the Mother shall be ever ready to face death. Do you think you would like to die when you think of the face of your daughter?"

"Do you think I can forget my daughter even if I do not see her?"

"If you cannot forget her, you should not join the Children."

"Must I believe that every Child that has joined this order has forgotten his wife and children? If so, then there can be but few Children in India!"

"Children are of two classes—those that are initiated and those that are not. Those that are not initiated are either house-holders or beggars. They present themselves only at times of warfare. They receive a certain portion of the spoils or are otherwise rewarded; and they retire. But those that are initiated have renounced all they hold dearest and nearest to their hearts. They are the leaders of the Order. I am not asking you to become an uninitiated Child. We have countless soldiers with *lathis* and spears. Unless you are initiated you can never be eligible for any serious work for the Children."

"What is initiation? Why should I have to be initiated? I have already taken the oath.

"You have to renounce that oath. You have to take a new oath from me."

"How can I renounce an oath?"

"I shall show you the way to a higher oath."

Chapter 5

WHEN Mahatma Satya entered the innermost shrine where the future of Mother India was most dazzlingly portrayed, he found another person beside Mahendra seated there, gently chanting the *Bande Mataram*. At the approach of Mahatma Satya the stranger stood up and bowed reverently. Mahatma Satya asked him, "Do you wish to be initiated?"

"I am awaiting your mercy, Master."

Then the Mahatma said to both Mahendra and the newcomer:

"Have you properly bathed, fasted and prayed?"

"Yes, Master."

"Do you swear before God and Mother India that you will obey all the laws of the Order of the Children?"

"Yes, indeed."

"Do you promise not to live the life of a householder until we win our victory?"

"We do."

"Will you forsake your father and mother?"

"Yes."
"Brothers and sisters?"
"We will."
"Wife and children?"
"Yes."
"Friends and relatives, servants and maids?"
"Yes."
"Wealth, property and enjoyment?"
"Yes, we renounce everything we have."

"Will you conquer your senses? Will you never even sit beside a woman? Will you observe strictest purity?"

"We will conquer our senses. We will never even sit with a woman. And we will observe strictest purity."

"Do you promise in the name of God and Mother India that you will not earn any money for yourself or for the members of your own families? That whatever you earn, you will donate to the treasury of the Children?"

"Yes, we will never earn money for ourselves or for our families. All we earn we promise to donate to the treasury of the Children."

"Will you take up arms to fight for the freedom of Mother India?"

"Yes, most decidedly we will."

"And never run away from the battlefield?"

"No, never."

"If you ever break your promises?"

"We shall enter burning flames or take poison or die fighting for the Mother."

"What of your caste? What caste do you belong to? I know Mahendra is a *Kshatrya*. What other caste do you belong to?"

"I am a Brahmin boy," the young man replied.

"Splendid! Do you both renounce your castes? For all Children belong to the same caste. In our work we do not differentiate between Hindu or Moslem, Buddhist or Sikh, Parsee or Pariah. We are all brothers here —all Children of the same Mother India. What do you say?"

"We agree to forget caste altogether. We all are Children of the same Mother."

"Now I am willing to initiate you. You must never break your promises. God and Mother India are your witnesses. Hell is the only fitting punishment for those who break their word of honor."

"Yes, we realize that indeed."

"Then sing the *Bande Mataram*."

They sang the *Bande Mataram* from the depths of their hearts. Then Mahatma Satya initiated them in the way that can never be revealed.

Chapter 6

AFTER the initiation Mahatma Satya led Mahendra to a secret chamber. There they sat face to face.

"Listen, my child," the Mahatma said, "from your initiation I infer that God is favorable to us. You are destined to do great deeds for the Mother. Please listen carefully to what I am about to tell you. Like Jiban and Bhavan, you will be excused from the need to roam about in the woods and fight. You must return to Padachina. Strange as it may seem, you will have to observe your vow of renunciation in your own home."

Mahendra was both sad and surprised to hear this; and yet he said not a word.

"Now," Mahatma Satya continued, "we are shelterless. If a powerful army surrounds us, we have no place where we can intrench ourselves. In other words, we do not have a fort. You have a splendid building, and you own the entire village. I want to build a fort there. If we surround the village with thick walls and mount guns upon them, we can build a formidable refuge. Please go home and live there. By degrees two thousand Children will follow you. You can utilize them for the building of the fort. Then build a house of solid iron. That will be the treasury of the Children. One by one, I shall send you the chests full of gold, silver and jewelry. You will use this wealth for the building of the fort. And I am gathering experts in the manufacture of arms. Upon their arrival establish a factory for the manufacture of cannon and rifles, gunpowder, shells and bullets. That's the reason why I ask you to return home immediately."

Mahendra agreed.

Chapter 7

MAHENDRA bowed low at Mahatma Satya's feet. Receiving the Master's blessings, he departed for Padachina. Then came the other disciple that was initiated with Mahendra. Mahatma Satya welcomed him cordially, and asked him to sit on the black deer-skin.

After talking for sometime in an agreeable manner, the Mahatma said: "Are you really deeply devoted to Mother India?"

"How can I say that?" the disciple replied. "What I call devotion may be mere hypocrisy or self-deception."

"Well said," the Mahatma responded approvingly. "Please think such thoughts and do such deeds that may daily deepen your devotion to the Mother. I bless you. Your efforts will be successful, for you are very young. My child, please tell me how should I call you?"

"Whatever you like, Master. I am only a servant of your servants."

"You are so young! So I shall call you Nabin.

Accept this as your name. But please tell me what was your name before? Tell me, even if you have objection to telling it to me. No one else will ever know what you tell me. The duties of the Children demand that even unmentionable things should be told to the *guru*. And no harm arises from that."

"My own name was Shantiram Devasharma."

"Villainous woman, your name was Shanti!" And the Mahatma pulled at the long black beard of the disciple. The false beard came off.

"Shame on you, little mother!" the Mahatma cried. "You were trying to deceive me. If you meant deception, then why such a long beard for such a young face? Even if you had a short beard, you could not hide your voice nor the glances of your eyes. If I were as stupid as that, do you think I would have undertaken this great work for the Mother?"

For a moment Shanti covered her face with her hands in shame; she then looked straight into the eyes of her Master, and said: "Master, what wrong have I done after all? Do you think that a woman can never have strength in her arms?"

"That can be compared only with the amount of water contained in the footprint of a cow!"

"Do you ever test the strength of your disciples?"

"Yes, indeed– Here, here is an iron bow, and here is a short iron wire. Attach this string to the bow. He who can do this is strong indeed!"

"Has every Child passed this test?" Shanti asked, as she examined the bow and the wire.

"No, by this we have only tested their strength."

"Has no one passed this test?"

"Yes, but only four."

"May I ask who they are?"

"There is no objection to that, I am one of them."

"Who are the rest?"

"Jiban, Bhavan and Jnan."

Shanti at once, and with little effort, attached the wire to the bow and threw the stringed bow at the Mahatma's feet.

Mahatma Satya was at once astonished, awe-struck and speechless. After a while he said:

"What! are you woman or goddess in disguise?"

"I am a humble woman: and I am chaste."

"Why so? Are you a widow? No, even a widow cannot acquire so much strength, for they eat only one meal a day."

"My husband is alive."

"Has he deserted you?"

"No, he has not, Master. I have come here in his quest."

Suddenly, as light emerges from behind a cloud, Mahatma Satya's memory flashed and he said:

"Yes, I do remember, the name of Jiban's wife was Shanti. Are you Jiban's wife?"

Shanti covered her face with the braids of her hair. Her face looked as if vines had fallen on a full-blown lotus blossom.

"Why are you bent on so sinful a deed here?" the Mahatma asked.

"A sinful deed! What do you mean?" Shanti spoke proudly, as she threw the braids on her back. "Is it a sin for a wife to join her husband in order to help him in his national duties? If the Children call this a sin, then their conception of sin is defective indeed! I am his helpmate and I am here to aid him. This is my religion and this is my duty!"

Mahatma Satya was pleased with Shanti's proud demeanor as she stood with her head high, neck curved and eyes glistening with rage.

"You are certainly a saintly woman," the Mahatma said. "But a wife is her husband's helpmate only in household duties; and not in heroic deeds."

"What hero ever became a hero without the co-operation of his wife?"

"Ordinary people are disturbed by a woman's love and attention. And this harms the pursuit of their duties. Hence the rule for the Children is never even to sit close to a woman. Jiban is my right arm! And you are here to cut off my right arm!"

"I am here to strengthen your right arm. I observe strictest continence. And I mean to remain a *brahmacharini* though living near my husband. I am here to perform the duties of the Children; and not to perform my duties of wifehood. I am not afflicted by separation from my husband. Then why should I not share his new duties with him? Hence I am here, Master; and I am here to stay."

"Well, my child, let me put you on probation for a few days."

Chapter 8

SHANTI, having been granted permission to stay at the *Ashram* that night, began looking for rooms. There were many empty ones. Gobardhan, an attendant, candle in hand, undertook to show them to her. She liked none of them. Gobardhan, in disappointment, turned to lead her back to the Mahatma.

"Brother Child," Shanti said, "we have not examined the rooms on the other side yet, you know."

"Those are very nice rooms indeed, but they are all occupied."

"Who stay there?"

"The most eminent generals."

"Who are those eminent generals?"

"Bhavan, Jiban, Dhiren and Jnan."

"Let us go and see those rooms."

Gobardhan led Shanti first to the room of Dhiren. Dhiren, busy reading the *Dronaparba* of the *Mahabharata*, was absorbed in thinking how Abhimanyu fought alone with seven warriors. He spoke not a word. Shanti, too, was silent, and left without speaking. She then entered Bhavan's room. He was engaged in his meditations and his gaze seemed fixed on a face. This face must have been that of Kalyani. He was so absorbed in his thoughts on the beauty and the grace of Kalyani's face that he did not even look at the face of Shanti.

Entering another room Shanti asked:

"Whose room is this?"

"This is Jiban's room," Gobardhan replied.

"Who is he? Why, no one is here!"

"He is a great general. He must be somewhere around. He will return presently."

"This is the best of all the rooms."

"But you can't have this room by any means."

"Why, may I ask?"

"Jiban lives here."

"He may find another room for himself."

"How is that possible? This is his room. He is all but the chief of this Home of the Mother. His orders are laws here. You don't know him. Oh, you certainly don't know him!"

"Then you may retire. If I cannot find a suitable room, I shall spend the night under a tree."

Gobardhan retired, and Shanti entered the room. She spread Jiban's black deerskin and sat herself on it. Then she brightened the little oil lamp, and began to read a book belonging to Jiban.

After a while Jiban returned. Though Shanti was dressed as a man, he knew her at sight.

"How strange that Shanti is here!" Jiban said.

"Who is Shanti, sir?" she asked as she slowly laid the book aside, and looked at Jiban's face.

Jiban was surprised beyond words. At last he mastered courage enough to say:

"You ask who Shanti is? Why, are you not Shanti?"

"I am Nabin, if you please," Shanti said haughtily, and she began to read the book again.

"This is certainly a joke to me," Jiban said laughing aloud. "But, then, Nabin, what brings you here in my room?"

"It is customary that when two gentlemen meet for the first time they should not fail to use words of respect like 'sir' and 'please.' I am not transgressing the rudiments of good manners amongst strangers. I do not see any reason why you should!"

"Thy command shall be most punctiliously observed, most honored Nabin," Jiban said in affected humility. "Now, this humble servant of thine begs thy permission to inquire as to why thou hast left Bharuipur and come here. This humble servant shall be most happy to know that."

"There is no excuse for irony either," Shanti said gravely. "I do not know Bharuipur. I came here to enter the order of the Children and I have been initiated today."

"Good gracious, is that true? This means ruination, I am sure."

"Why ruination? You, too, are initiated, aren't you?"

"But you are a woman!"

"What do you mean by that? What makes you say so?"

"Most respected lady, I was always under the impression that my wife was a woman."

"Wife! Have you a wife?"

"I thought I had one."

"And you are under the impression that I am your wife?"

"I am absolutely sure of that."

"If such a ludicrous thought has made its appearance in your consciousness, then, pray tell me what should be your duty?"

"To deprive you of your garment of deerskin by force; and then to drink the nectar from your lips."

"You must be either insane or under the influence of narcotic hemp. Did you not, at the time of your initiation, take the oath that you would have nothing to do with women? Well, if you really think that I am a woman, then you should not come near me and you should not even speak to me."

And Shanti began to read the book again. Thus vanquished, Jiban prepared a separate bed for himself and retired for the night.

Book 3

Chapter 1

THE new year dawned happily. God smiled again on India. In Bengal rain fell copiously. Crops became abundant. The living had enough to eat; but those that were sick and famished through starvation were unable to tolerate food and died. The famine areas were lacking in population. In the villages home after home became merely a hunting-ground for ghosts and a resting-place for cattle. Hundreds of farms remained fallow and soon became covered with jungle. On all sides the jungle abounded. The smiling farms, the green pastures and the pleasure gardens of the young men and young women of the villages fast turned into dense forest.

Three years passed, and still the jungles grew. Places once inhabited by human beings now became infested with ferocious tigers; quarters that had once resounded with the music of the ornaments and with the lilt of the laughter of happy women, now became dens where bears reared their cubs; places where once children had laughed, had sung and danced with joy, were now the camping grounds of herds of wild elephants tearing at trunks of trees. Temples became homes for jackals and owls; and within the music rooms of the past, venomous snakes trapped frogs in bright daylight. Crops were plentiful, but there were not people enough for the food; no customers to buy the grain. The farmer could not pay his taxes to the landlord, and the British Raj began to confiscate the landlords' holdings. The owners of land became poor. Homes everywhere became poverty-stricken. Men lived by looting. Thieves and bandits were active again. Honest people protected themselves within their own homes.

The Children, however, were on the move once more and began a campaign of seizing rifles and revolvers.

"Comrades, if on the one hand," Bhavan said to the Children, "you find a room full of diamonds and rubies, pearls and sapphires, and on the other a broken rifle—lay aside the precious stones, but by all means return to our Mother's *Ashram* with the rifle."

The Children sent their agents to the villages to make converts, and freely divided their spoils with the new disciples. Thus enticed, the number of Children in the villages grew by leaps and bounds. Each day hundreds, each month thousands of recruits added to the strength of the Children who swore allegiance to the Mother at the feet of Bhavan and Jiban. The Children were inspired with new courage. They began to attack British officials at sight; nor on occasion did they hesitate to kill them. They began to loot English treasuries whenever and wherever possible in order to enrich the Children's treasury.

The local British authorities became impatient and sent company after company of sepoys to punish the Children. But the Children were organized now into military companies, efficiently armed and proud of their prowess. The sepoys failed even to gain ground against them. In every encounter the superior forces of the Children defeated the sepoys amidst shouts of *Bande Mataram*. If by chance a company of Children was forced to yield before the sepoys, immediately another company appeared on the scene, vanquished the victors, and shouted *Bande Mataram* as they marched away.

At that time the notorious Warren Hastings was Governor-General of British India, but even he shook with fear at the Children's shouts of *Bande Mataram*. At first he tried to quell the rebellion with the help of local sepoys. But these were treated so roughly by the Children, that they ran for their lives if they heard the words *Bande Mataram* being uttered even by old women. Frustrated, Hastings was at last forced to send a company of sepoys of the East India Company, under the leadership of a Captain Thomas, to crush the Children.

Upon his arrival at the scene of the rebellion, Captain Thomas made elaborate arrangements for his campaign. He gathered together the local and the provincial sepoys, and mingled with them his own expert soldiers. He divided this mixed command into different companies, placing each company under an experienced and efficient officer. He marked out the territory into different sections; and ordered his captains to advance, each combing his section thoroughly for the rebels, with instructions to slaughter them at sight like rabbits. Some of the soldiers of the East India Company became drunk with rum; others became intoxicated with hemp; all, however, fixed their bayonets and were eager to kill the Children. But the Children were countless in number, and by this time invincible. Like a field of wheat before the farmer's scythe, the soldiers of Captain Thomas were cut down. And shouts of *Bande Mataram* deafened the captain's ears.

Chapter 2

IN those days in Bengal the East India Company owned a great many silk factories. There was a large factory at Shibgram with an Englishman named Dunniworth as manager. The Company made excellent provision for the protection of the factories, and that is the reason why Mr. Dunniworth had managed to save his life. He felt compelled however to send his wife and children to Calcutta, leaving himself to be harassed by the Children.

Captain Thomas encamped at Shibgram with a few companies of his soldiers. Encouraged by the example of the Children, a group of pariahs had begun to seize other people's properties by force. Once a huge wagon full of flour and butter, rice and poultry was approaching the camp of Captain Thomas. The new pariah bandits could not resist the temptation to seize such a prize, but they were beaten off by the soldiers. The victorious captain at once sent reports to headquarters at Calcutta saying that that very day with the help of only 157 sepoys he had defeated 14,700 rebels; 2,153 of whom had been killed, 1,223 wounded, and seven taken prisoner. Only the last item of the report was really true; but the captain felt as if he had won the battle of Blenheim. His excessive pride in this achievement caused him to strut about with the air of a conqueror. And so he advised Mr. Dunniworth:

"I have quelled the rebellion. Now you may send for your wife and children at Calcutta."

"Splendid advice indeed," Mr. Dunniworth answered. "But, please stay here for another ten days. Let the country get quieter still, and then I shall send for them."

Mr. Dunniworth's pantry was full of rare and delicious foodstuffs, and he had an expert cook. So Captain Thomas cheerfully began to take the fullest advantage of Mr. Dunniworth's hospitality.

Bhavan, on the other hand, was becoming impatient to conquer Captain Thomas, and thus acquire the title of Sambarari II. "We are sure to destroy these alien aggressors some day," Bhavan said to himself. "Let them gather together as they grow in number. We must stay away from them, and they will grow even more careless." So the Children did not display even a sign of their existence. And the Captain ate and drank plentifully and slept well.

Captain Thomas was exceedingly fond of hunting. Occasionally he ventured forth into the jungles around Shibgram. He was a fearless man. In strength and courage he was unrivalled among the English in India. Once he was out hunting on horseback with Mr. Dunniworth and a group of hunters. The dense jungle he chose was dangerously infested with tigers, bears and wild buffalo. The group penetrated far into it. At last the hunters refused to go any further, for all paths in the jungle had ended. Mr. Dunniworth, who had once been attacked by a tiger in these very forests, also refused to proceed.

The Captain, having sent them all back, alone entered further into the wilderness. As there were no paths, his horse balked; so he placed his rifle on his shoulder, left the horse and proceeded on foot. He looked all around for tigers, but failed to find any. Instead he found something quite different—a young holyman seated under a huge tree almost wrapped by creepers and foliage laden with full-blown flowers. The young man was radiantly beautiful. The glow of his face added a lustre to the flowers. Captain Thomas was surprised. Surprise was quickly followed by anger. He knew a little Bengali, so in that language he asked:

"Who are you?"

"I am an ascetic," the *sanyasi* replied.

"Are you a rebel?"

"What is a rebel?"

"I am going to shoot you."

"Kill me, I have no objection."

At such a reply, the Captain was hesitant whether to shoot or not. Just at that moment the *sanyasi* fell like lightning upon the Englishman and snatched his rifle away from him. Then he dropped the skin from around his body, and the matted locks of hair from his head.

And the English captain found himself confronted by a ravishingly beautiful Hindu woman.

"Look here, Englishman, I am a woman; to say nothing of a human being, I do not hurt even a creeper. So do not be afraid of your life. But I want to tell you that this country belongs to us. This is our Motherland. We are the children of this soil. You have no more moral or legal right to rule over this country than we have to rule over your England. Why don't you Englishmen, like true Christians, return peacefully to your own homeland?"

"Who are you?"

"You see, I am a female *sanyasi*. I am the wife of one of those heroes of India with whom you have come to fight."

"Will you stay in my house?"

"As your mistress, I suppose!"

"You may stay as my wife—but there won't be any marriage."

"I had a silver-colored monkey. It died recently. The cage is empty. I shall tie you with a nice chain around your waist. Will you stay in that empty cage as my pet monkey, Englishman? And we grow delicious bananas in our garden. I shall give you plenty of bananas to eat."

"You are a very spirited woman, I see. I am pleased with your courage. You had better come to my house. Your husband will die in the war. What will happen to you then?"

"Then let us come to this understanding. War is inevitable. It is now only a matter of days. If you win the war and if I am alive after the war is over, I agree to live as your mistress. And if we win, will you live in my monkey cage and eat bananas as a monkey?"

"I love to eat bananas. Have you any now with you?"

"Here, you had better take back your rifle! It is difficult to talk with such savages!"

Shanti dropped the rifle, and walked away smiling.

Chapter 3

LIKE a light-footed doe in the jungle Shanti disappeared from view. And in a little while Captain Thomas heard a woman's voice sing:

"My Lord, my Lord,
Who can stem the turbulent tide of youth?"

And from somewhere else in the woods sang out that melodious instrument called the *sarengi*. It was rendering the same song. In a moment a male voice took up the melody:

"My Lord, my Lord,
Who can stem the turbulent tide of youth?"

Then the three strains sang in unison, and Shanti walked as she sang:

"My Lord, my Lord,
Who can stem the turbulent tide of youth?
The tide is on
And my new boat sails joyous;
The captain is at the helm,

My Lord, my Lord,
Let me brush aside
These embankments of sand
And reach the land of my heart's desire.
The tide is on the swelling stream
My Lord, my Lord,
Who can stem the turbulent tide of youth?"

The human voices stopped singing and the *sarengi* sang alone:

"My Lord, my Lord,
The tide is on the swelling stream
Who can stem the tide on the swelling stream?"

Shanti slowly entered the very heart of the jungle. No one from outside might ever see what lay inside this wilderness of darkness—a little cottage hidden by the branches and the foliage of the trees, the roof made of leaves. Twigs of trees served as strings. The floor was of wood covered with earth. Shanti opened the door of creepers, and entered the cottage. Jiban was playing the *sarengi* there.

"You come here after such a long time, Shanti?" Jiban said. "Is it high tide in the river again?"

"Dead pools are never affected with the rising tide in the rivers, you know," Shanti said as she laughed.

Jiban was disappointed at the reply, and said:

"Look here, Shanti, for the sin of breaking my vow but once, I have to pay with my life. That penalty must be paid. It is only at your request that I have not yet paid it. But a fierce battle cannot be long delayed. On that battlefield I must pay the penalty. I have to die—and I must die then. The day of my death is here! But—."

"I am your wife in the faith," Shanti interrupted. "It is my religion to help you in the performance of your duties. You have accepted a serious religion. I left home only to help you in the path of your duty. I am roaming in these jungles so that you and I together may serve Mother India to the best of our ability. I want to fortify you in the discharge of your duties as a Child. As a wife in the faith, how can I stand in the way of your higher duties? Marriage is for this life as well as for the next. Let us imagine that the earthly part of the marriage was not meant to be ours. Our marriage is only for the life beyond death. We shall thus reap a double harvest for our unflinching loyalty to our duties. But why speak of the supreme atonement? What sin have you committed? You promised not to live with a woman. And you have not done that. Then why do you talk of penalty, and of death, my most beloved? You are my teacher. How can I teach you the way of the *dharma*? You are a hero; and how can I teach you the duties of a hero?"

"Shanti, you have just taught me a great lesson," Jiban said with tears in his eyes. "And yet, our marriage in this life has not been in vain either. You love me and I love you. Can any one expect anything higher than that from a marriage on earth? So sing *Bande Mataram*, and forget all sorrows in the supreme joy of that song."

Fervently, they both sang together.

Chapter 4

ON one of those days Bhavan went to the town. And there he left a broad street to enter a dark and narrow lane. High buildings stood on both sides of the lane. Only at noon could the sunlight strike the lane and then but for a moment. At all other hours darkness was supreme.

Bhavan entered a two-story building on the lane and walked into the kitchen. A middle-aged woman was cooking there. She was fat and dark, dressed in pure white as a widow. Noisily she was stirring rice. She was talking aloud to herself, and making grimaces.

"Good morning, grandma cook," Bhavan said. She was taken aback to see Bhavan, and began fixing her dress. So fat was she that an ordinary *sari* was too short for the proper veiling of her face. In a mood of embarrassment she said:

"Bhavan, I see. You are most welcome. But why do you use such polite language with me?"

"You are our grandma."

"You are very affectionate to call me grandma. You are a holyman. Well, well, may you live long—that is, you may call me grandma—at any rate I am much older than you are."

Gouri was in fact about twenty-five years older than he, but the clever Bhavan said:

"What do you mean, grandma? I call you grandma because you are such a romantic young lady! Don't you remember that you were six years my junior the last time we made the calculation? I feel as if I must ask the permission of the leader of our Order to get married to you. I came here today only to say this to you."

"You should never say such things! I am a widow, you know."

"Do you mean to imply that I can't marry you?"

"Well, you may do just as you please. You are a learned man, and I am a woman of no education. What do I understand about these things? But—then—when do you think we should get married?"

"I must meet the leader of our order first.—But, by the way, how is Kalyani?" Bhavan strained every nerve to restrain his laughter.

Gouri looked hurt. She suspected the sincerity of Bhavan and at once came to the conclusion that he was only joking with her. So she said rather indifferently:

"She is all right, as usual."

"Please go upstairs and tell her that I am here and want to see her."

In one of the rooms upstairs a beautiful woman sat on a torn mat. But at the moment the woman's beauty was somewhat veiled by a deep shadow, like the dark and mysterious shadow of a cloud at noon on the breast of a full river singing songs of joy. Waves were disturbing the breast of the river, and on the shores branches of trees were bent low with the burden of full-blown blossoms waving to and fro in the wind. Rows of boats were disturbing the smoothness of the river. It was noon, and yet the beauty of the river was enveloped in gloom. So it was with the face of this woman. Her hair was just as dark and as restlessly beautiful as before; her eyebrows were as delicately painted in a bow, as if with a brush, as before; her eyes were as picturesquely large, as brightly black, and as eloquently glistening as before. Her glances were not as ravishing and sensuous but they were serenely gentle. Her lips were as intensely bright as before. In unruffled contentment her heaving breast responded rhythmically to her breath. Her arms were graceful and richly soft. But today that freshness, that radiance, that striking restlessness and that sensuousness were no more. In other words, the freshness of youth had gone. But beauty was there; and grace too. She had now acquired ripeness of dignity and contentment. Before, she had looked like the most beautiful of all women on earth; now she looked like the accursed angel born on earth. Around her a few religious books were scattered and the walls of the room were covered with various religious pictures.

"Kalyani, are you well—physically?" Bhavan asked as he entered the room.

"Will you never cease to ask me that question?"

Kalyani replied. "My physical welfare is of no use to you or to me."

"The man who plants a tree and waters it every day is happy indeed to see the tree grow. I planted life in your dead body. Why should I not inquire how the tree is growing now?"

"Does the poison tree ever wither?"

"Is life a poison?"

"Otherwise why did I want to put an end to it by taking what was like nectar to me?"

"I have been thinking, for a long time, of asking you that question. But I could never summon courage enough to do so. Please tell me, who poisoned your life?"

"No one poisoned my life," Kalyani replied with the utmost serenity. "Life itself is poisonous. My life is poisonous. Your life is poisonous. The lives of all human beings are poisonous!"

"Yes, Kalyani, my life is poisonous indeed! From the day–. By the way, have you finished the grammar?"

"No."

"The dictionary?"

"I don't like it."

"You were so anxious to study before! What makes you indifferent now?"

"When a great scholar like you can be such a sinner, it is better not to study at all. What is the news of my husband, my Lord?"

"Why do you ask that same question over and over again? He is dead, as far as you are concerned."

"I am dead to him, but not he to me."

"You committed suicide so that he might be dead to you too. Why do you repeat the same thing so persistently, Kalyani?"

"Does death ever put an end to kinship? How is he, pray?"

"He is well."

"Where is he? Is he at Padachina?"

"He is still there."

"What is he doing now?"

"The same thing as before. He is building a fort and manufacturing arms and ammunition. Today thousands of the Children are well armed with the arms he has manufactured. It is due to his endeavors that we no longer need guns, rifles and ammunition. Among the Children he stands paramount. He is the supreme source of our strength today."

"All this would have been impossible if I were alive! The man who has a stone tied to his neck can never swim. The man who has chains around his feet can never run. Why, O holyman, why did you save my useless life?"

"A wife is called her husband's co-religionist. She helps him in the discharge of his duties."

"In small affairs, yes. But in duties of major importance, she is a hindrance. I took poison only to brush myself away from the path of his duties. And you, a sinner of a holyman, you villain, why, why did you give me back my life?"

"Well, Kalyani, let what I gave you stay as my very own. Will you give me the life I gave to you?"

"Do you know how my daughter, Sukumari, is?"

"I have not had any news of her for a long time. Jiban has not been home."

"Can you not get me any news of my daughter? I have to give up my husband. But while alive, why should I give up my child? It would make me happy to find my daughter at this precarious time. But, why should you do so much for me?"

"I shall indeed, I shall fetch your child to you, dearest Kalyani. But then—what?"

"What do you mean by that?"

"How about the husband?"

"Of my own wish I have given him up."

"If he attains the summit of his quest?"

"Then I will be his again. Does he know that I am alive?"

"No."

"Do you ever see him?"

"Yes."

"Does he ever speak of me?"

"No. What relationship can a husband have with a wife that is dead?"

"What do you mean by that?"

"You may marry again. You have been born anew."

"Please bring my daughter to me."

"Yes, I shall. You may marry again, I say."

"Marry you; perhaps that's what you mean!"

"Will you marry again?"

"Marry you?"

"Suppose that is the case."

"What will happen to your vows as a Child?"

"My vows may go to the devil!"

"How about the life after death?"

"That may go to the devil also."

"And the sublime mission of your life?"

"That too may go to the devil."

"Why do you want to make all these tremendous sacrifices?"

"For you, Kalyani; and for you alone! Listen Kalyani: Be he man or Mahatma, master or *deva*, mind is ever unconquerable. The duties of the Children are my life, but let me tell you for the first time that you are more precious than my life or my salvation. The day I brought you back to life I sacrificed my all at your feet. I never knew that such beauty could exist on this earth! If I had ever suspected that I were to look upon such a beautiful woman, I would never have joined the Order of the Children. All my sense of duty has been burnt to ashes by the fire of your beauty. Only my life has been left me. And for these last four years, that life too has been burnt into charcoal. I cannot stand it any longer, Kalyani. My heart, mind and body are on fire. On fire, Kalyani, yes, on fire. Fire burns, and yet the fuel is all but gone, yes, all but gone, my dearest Kalyani. I am hungry for your love. I am thirsty for your divine embrace. For you, Kalyani, and for you alone, I have endured this excruciating torture for four long years. I can stand it no longer.—I cannot, Kalyani, I cannot—"

"You have told me yourself that the code of the Children demands death as an atonement for the Child who has been conquered by the craving of the senses. Is that not true?"

"Yes, that is true, absolutely, true!"

"Then the atonement for your sin is death?"

"The only atonement for me is death."

"Will you die if I fulfill your desires?"

"Certainly, I will die."

"And if I do not fulfill your desires?"

"Then, too, death is my atonement; for my mind has been overcome by lust. Death, and death alone can atone for my sin."

"Then I refuse to fulfill your desires. When do you think you will die?"

"In the fight that is imminent."

"Then you may go now. Will you send my daughter to me?"

"Yes, I shall. But, Kalyani, will you remember me when I am dead?"

"Yes, I shall ever remember you, but as a sinner; and as a fallen Child of the Mother."

Bhavan walked out of the room; and Kalyani sat down to read the scriptures.

Chapter 5

DEEPLY engrossed in thought Bhavan walked towards the *Ashram*. Night overtook him as he entered the woods. Suddenly he noticed that some one was walking ahead of him.

"Who goes there?" Bhavan asked.

"If you only knew how to ask the question!"

"Bande."

"Mataram."

"My name is Bhavan."

"I am Dhiren."

"Dhiren! What brings you here now?"

"I was looking for you."

"Why?"

"I have something to tell you."

"What is it, Dhiren?"

"On that subject I can speak to you only privately."

"Why not say it now. We are by ourselves here."

"Did you go to the town?"

"Yes."

"To Gouridevi's house?"

"Did you go to the town too?"

"A very beautiful woman lives there."

Bhavan was surprised and felt a little fear on hearing this. He said:

"What are you talking about?"

"Did you meet her?" Dhiren asked.

"And if I did?"

"You are infatuated with that woman."

"Dear Dhiren, what makes you ask about all these things? What you say is absolutely true. But how many beside you know about this?"

"No one else."

"Then I can free myself of this disgrace by killing you."

"Yes, you can."

"Then come, let us fight in this solitary place. Either I free myself of this disgrace by killing you, or you kill me to relieve me from the gnawing pains of my heart. Have you weapons for a fight?"

"Yes, I have. Would I dare to talk to you about these things unarmed? If you have decided on a duel, I am willing. The Children are not allowed to fight among themselves; but fight only in self-defense. But do you not think it would be better for us to begin fighting after you have listened to the full story?"

"There is no harm in that." Bhavan said, and he placed his sword on Dhiren's shoulder, so that he might not run away.

"Why don't you marry Kalyani?" Dhiren asked.

"Kalyani! So you even know her name!"

"Why don't you marry her?"

"She has a husband; and the Children cannot marry."

"The Children's creed can be renounced, for all I know. You are dying for love! Careful, you are cutting my shoulder deeply!"

"What brought you here to suggest such sinful advice? You must have some selfish interest behind this infamous proposition."

"I intend to tell you that too. But, please, do not press your sword so hard on my shoulder. The duties of the Children have taxed my patience beyond endurance. I am sick and tired of them. I want to leave the Order. I am impatient to spend the rest of my days with my wife and children. I must leave the Order. But how can I return home and live in peace? I am well known as a rebel. If I return home, the British will cut my head off; or the Children will kill me as a traitor. So I want you to go my way."

"Why do you choose me?"

"Ah, that's the crux of the question. The Children are under your command. Mahatma Satya is not here now. You are the commander-in-chief of the forces of the Children. I am absolutely certain that you will win the war if you fight with your soldiers. Now, when you win the war, why not establish a kingdom in your own name. The soldiers will obey you. You be the King and let Kalyani be your Queen. I shall ever remain a humble servant of yours and thus pass my days in the company of my wife and children. And I shall bless you for having disbanded the Children altogether."

"Dhiren," Bhavan said, as he withdrew his sword. "Fight. I must kill you. I may live as a slave to my senses; but I am not a traitor. You are a traitor; and you are enticing me to be a traitor. I commit no sin if I kill you. I must kill you, villain, I must kill you."

Scarcely had Bhavan finished his say than Dhiren ran off as fast as he could. Bhavan followed, but searched for him in vain.

Chapter 6

UPON his arrival at the *Ashram*, Bhavan entered a deep forest. In a certain part of the jungle were the ruins of an ancient building. On the bricks and stones of the ruins grew thorny creepers and dense brush. Countless serpents lived there. One of the broken courtyards was less dilapidated than the others, and cleaner. Bhavan chose that spot to sit.

He plunged into deep thought. The night was intensely dark. The forest was endless and impregnable even for wild animals. It was forlorn and quiet. The only noise one could hear was the distant howl of tigers, or the fearful cries of hunger or fear of other animals. Now and then there was the sound of the wings of huge birds in the trees. Amidst these desolate ruins Bhavan sat alone. The world was all but dead to him. With his hands on his temples he sat in deep thought. He was breathless, motionless and fearless.

"I have to face my own destiny," he said to himself. "There is no escape from that. I am sorry, however, that

I was so scandalously swept into the currents of passion and desire. My body may perish in a moment and the passions of the senses perish with the body. And yet I was so overpowered by my senses! I am a traitor to my sense of duty. Death is better for me than to live this life of shame and disgrace. Shame, shame on me; I must die."

Just at that moment an owl cried far overhead:

"What is that noise?" Bhavan spoke aloud. "I hear the call of death. Death calls me! Tell me, tell me, O thou Infinite Spirit, tell me who has ordained my death. I know you are the mystic Word. But I cannot decipher the meaning of your mystic message of command. Please protect me from sin. Please lead me into the path of virtue. Yes, my Mahatma and my Master, lead me, lead me—I beg of you—lead me into the path of my duty—my duty to Mother India."

Just then Bhavan was startled to hear his Master's own voice say sweetly and deeply:

"Thou shalt never more stray away from the path of thy duty—I bless thee, Bhavan!

Bhavan's hair stood on end. He shouted like a child at the top of his voice:

"What, this is my Mahatma's voice! Oh, my master, where are you? Please let me see you now. I need you, yes, I do need you at this time!"

But no one appeared; and no one spoke another word. Bhavan called out repeatedly; but there was no answer to his supplication.

When at dawn the morning sun smiled on the tops

of the trees, Bhavan returned to the *Ashram*. He heard some one sing the *Bande Mataram*. And in a moment he recognized the voice of the Mahatma. Evidently Mahatma Satya had returned from his pilgrimage.

Chapter 7

WHEN Jiban had gone out of the cottage, Shanti again picked up the *sarengi* and sang most sweetly, most feelingly:

"Mother, hail!
Thou with sweet springs flowing,
Thou fair fruits bestowing,
Cool with zephyrs blowing,
Green with corn-crops growing,
Mother, hail!"

As if in reply to Shanti's song, someone from outside sang resonantly in a deep voice:

"Though now three hundred million voices through thy mouth sonorous shout,
Though twice three hundred million hands hold thy trenchant sword-blades out,
Yet with all this power now,
Mother, wherefore powerless thou?"

In an instant Shanti was reverently bowing at the feet of Mahatma Satya.

"Master," she said, "for what good deeds of mine am I thus rewarded by your august presence? Please command what I have to do. I seek your blessing."

"Mother, I bless you. Nothing but good can befall you."

"How is that possible, Master, when you have ordained widowhood for me?"

"I certainly failed to appreciate your real worth. Mother, without fully realizing the strength of the rope, I pulled it too hard. You are wiser than I. You must find a way out of the tangle for me. Please do not let Jiban know that I know the truth about you. He may continue to live for your love, as he has been doing for sometime. We can win only if he lives."

"Well, Master," Shanti said, her black eyes darker in flashing anger, "my husband and I are two halves of the same soul. I am going to report to him our entire conversation. If he has to die, let him die. I lose nothing by his death; for I am sure to die with him. He will attain heaven indeed; and do you think any one can keep me away from wherever he is?"

"I have never met with defeat. Today I acknowledge my defeat at your hands. Mother, I am your child. Please have mercy on this child of yours. I beg of you, please, save the life of Jiban; and save your own life too. Thus, and thus alone can I win success—yes, win freedom for our enslaved Mother India!"

"My husband's duties are in his hands," Shanti said and laughed. "Who am I to hold him from the discharge of his duties? In this life the husband is the lord of the wife; but in the life beyond death, righteousness is the lord of us all. My husband is great indeed to me; but greater than he is my sense of duty; and greater even than that is the sense of duty of my husband. I can sacrifice my sense of duty as I like, but I can never allow myself to cause my husband to stray from his path of duty. Mahatma, that is impossible! If my husband has to die at your command, let him die. I can never, never ask him not to die."

"Mother, there must be sacrifice for our unflinching devotion to the cause," Mahatma Satya said with a sigh. "We all shall have to sacrifice ourselves. I am going to die. Jiban and Bhavan will have to die. Perhaps, my little mother, you, too, will have to die. But you must realize that we must die doing our duty. There is no sense in dying merely for the sake of death, without furthering the cause of our country's freedom. Hitherto I have addressed only my Mother India as mother; for we recognize no other mother than our Motherland— with sweet springs flowing, fair fruits bestowing, cool with zephyrs blowing, green with corn crops growing. Today I address you as mother. So do honor your child's request. Please do your very best to win victory— and— save Jiban's life, and your own."

Mahatma Satya left the cottage singing the *Bande Mataram*.

Chapter 8

GRADUALLY it became known among the Children that Mahatma Satya had returned to the *Ashram;* and that he had asked the Children to meet in the *Ashram* grounds to hear an important message. So groups of Children began to gather, and before long ten thousand of them had assembled in the forest by the river.

The vast forest was full of mango, palm, banyan, sal and other trees. Every one was happy and shouted with joy to hear of the return of the Mahatma. The rank and file of the Children did not know where he had gone, nor for what purpose. It was rumored, however, that he had gone to the Himalayas for prayers and meditation for the welfare of the Children. And thus they all whispered into one another's ears:

"The Mahatma's prayers have been answered. We are sure to defeat the British and win back the sovereignty of our country."

Louder and louder they shouted *Bande Mataram.*

Yes, ten thousand Children shouted *Bande Mataram* at the top of their voices. The trees were rustling in the winds, the river was singing, the moon and the stars were shining brightly in the blue sky, where here and there pieces of white cloud floated carelessly by. Green trees towered over green earth. White beds of sand bordered the translucent stream. The entire length of the river bank was covered with flowers of every kind.

Amidst deafening shouts of *Bande Mataram*, Mahatma Satya appeared. Bathed bright in the moonbeams that filtered through the leaves, ten thousand Children bowed on the soft green grass to do homage to him.

"May God, who is great, bless you with success," Mahatma Satya said loudly, lifting both his hands to bless the assembled Children. "May He grant strength to your arms, devotion to your mind and unalloyed consecration on your part to our beloved Mother India. Now let us sing the *Bande Mataram*."

And they all sang the *Bande Mataram* together. The song over, Mahatma Satya blessed them again, and continued:

"My beloved Children! Listen closely. I have something very important to tell you tonight. Captain Thomas of England, that villain and assassin, has massacred numerous Children. Tonight we shall destroy him with all his soldiers. This is the command of God. What do you say?"

The answer came in the form of a spontaneous shout, a fierce *Bande Mataram* that rent the skies and shook the forest all around.

"Yes, indeed," shouted a leader from the crowd, "we must destroy the British soldiers and their Captain instantly. Just tell us where they are, and the task will be shortly over. Tell us where they are!"

"Kill, kill the British soldiers," shouted a second, "yes, kill them all; for they have killed too many of our patriots." Words like these echoed from the distant mountain sides.

"We have to be patient," Mahatma Satya said, "so that we may do our duties successfully. The British have cannon. It is impossible for us to fight with them without cannon. Moreover, they are a heroic race. Seventeen cannon are on the way to us from our fort at Padachina. When these arrive we will march out to fight the enemy. Look, it is dawning in the East! Probably within a few hours—but hear—what is that? What do I hear?"

Suddenly, cannon roared simultaneously on all sides of the woods. But they were British cannon that thundered. Captain Thomas had surrounded the forest and sought to kill the Children like fish trapped in a net.

Chapter 9

"Boom, boom, boom" roared the English cannon. From the depths of the forest the echoes came back, "boom, boom, boom." The terrific roar traveled along the river banks, and the distant horizon resounded. The sound entered the forest beyond the river, and again roared out "boom, boom, boom." Mahatma Satya commanded:

"Find out whose guns those are!"

Several Children jumped on their horses, and raced to gather the information. No sooner had they emerged from the woods than British bullets rained on them in torrents; and they instantly dropped, their horses under them. Mahatma Satya, seeing all this from a distance, ordered:

"Climb the trees and see what is happening."

Jiban had already climbed one of the tallest trees, and was watching in the morning rays of the sun. He said:

"Those are English guns, Master."

"Is it cavalry or infantry?"

"Both."

"How strong?"

"I cannot guess yet, for they are still emerging from the wood."

"Are they English soldiers, or sepoys?"

"Mostly English soldiers."

"Come down from the tree, Jiban."

Jiban came down and Mahatma Satya spoke:

"Jiban, we have ten thousand Children present; see what you can do. You are General today."

Jiban garbed himself like a soldier and mounted his horse. He looked into the eyes of Nabin and signalled without a word. Nabin, too, spoke with an eloquent glance. No one present could understand the message that passed between them. Perhaps only those two could guess in their hearts that this was their last farewell on earth. Then Nabin lifted her right arm, and said:

"Comrades, let us sing the *Bande Mataram*."

The Children sang the *Bande Mataram* so loudly that the song seemed to drown even the cannons' roar. Just then they began to feel the volley of British bullets and cannon balls. Some died and others fell wounded. And yet they kept on singing the *Bande Mataram*. The song over, everyone became silent. Save for the thunder of the English cannon, and the rattling of swords, the entire forest was quiet.

Then, piercing this silence, Mahatma Satya shouted:

"God will shower His blessings on you—how far are the cannon?"

"Only a little meadow adjoining these woods separates them from us," said a voice from a tree.

"Who is it that speaks?"

"I am Nabin, Master."

"You are ten thousand strong," said the Mahatma to the Children around him, "and you must win. Capture the guns from the British by the double force of body and soul."

"Forward, comrades, forward, we must advance without fear!" shouted Jiban from his horse.

On foot and on horseback ten thousand Children followed Jiban. The Children on foot had rifles on their backs; swords hung from their waists, and they carried spears in their hands. But no sooner had they emerged from the shelter of the woods than they were torn to pieces by an incessant shower of English bullets and cannon balls. Many Children thus died without a chance to fight.

"Jiban, what is the use of this useless slaughter?" some one said from behind.

Jiban turned back to see Bhavan, and asked:

"What do you think we should do, Bhavan?"

"Let us protect the lives of the Children from behind trees. In an open field, and unarmed with cannon, we can not stand them off even for a moment; but we can continue our fight for a long time from behind cover."

"You are right, Bhavan, but the Master has ordered the capture of the English cannon."

"It is impossible to capture them; but if we have to proceed, you had better stay behind—let me go forward."

"No, Bhavan, that won't do. I must face death today!"

"No, Jiban, it is I who must die today. I must make atonement, you know. You are sinless, Jiban! There can be no atonement for you. My mind is shameful, and I must die. You stay behind, but let me rush to embrace death."

"Bhavan, I do not know anything about your sin. But I do know that if you live, the Children are sure to win. So, let me go forward to court death as atonement."

For a moment Bhavan said nothing. He then weighed these words between his lips:

"If I have to die, let me die today. It is right to die the day one has to die. There is no such thing as time with death."

"If you insist so persistently, Bhavan, then take the lead Brother, take the lead."

Bhavan at once rushed to the head of the army. The Children were being mowed down right and left, their bodies torn to pieces. They were falling headlong in heaps of human flesh and blood. Enraged at this sight, Bhavan shouted:

"We must plunge ourselves into these waves of blood—who dare, comrades, Children, who dare? Chant the hymn of the Mother—sing, sing the *Bande Mataram.*"

And the Children sang the *Bande Mataram* loudly as if to defy the English guns.

Chapter 10

SINGING the *Bande Mataram* the Children lifted their spears and rushed the English artillery. The enemy guns and rifles played havoc with them. They were cut to bits, torn to pieces, pierced through their bodies. Those who remained alive were exceedingly disorganized; and yet, not a Child turned back.

In the meantime, Captain Thomas ordered a group of sepoys with fixed bayonets to charge the Children to the right. The attack was sudden and fierce. Attacked from two directions the Children, even under the leadership of Bhavan, became discouraged. Every minute hundreds of them were giving their lives fighting for the freedom of the Motherland.

"Bhavan, you were right," Jiban said. "There is no use continuing this slaughter any longer. Let us slowly retreat."

"How can we retreat now?" Bhavan asked. "That is impossible. Complete annihilation will follow retreat at this time."

"We are being attacked from the front and the right. The left is open to us; so let us slowly turn left and retreat that way."

"How can we retreat that way. There lies the river. The water is high and its current strong. Do you mean to escape from English guns only to drown our soldiers in the river?"

"But there is a bridge across the river."

"If we try to cross by that little bridge, destruction is ours, I am certain."

"We may do this: The courage and generalship you have displayed in this battle are superhuman. Nothing is impossible with you. So you keep a handful of men to protect the vanguard. And under cover of your soldiers, let me cross the bridge with the majority of the rest. Those that are left with you are sure to die, but those I am taking away from here might, yes, might survive to fight in the future."

"A splendid idea indeed! Let me advance at once."

So with two thousand warriors, Bhavan made a desperate dash towards the English artillery, shouting *Bande Mataram* fervently. A ferocious battle ensued in this section. But how long could the Children withstand the onslaught? They were being mowed down mercilessly.

Jiban, on the other hand, turned slightly to the left and moved towards the bridge along the edge of the forest. But from a distance Lieutenant Watson of Captain Thomas' regiment noticed this clever move. So he rallied some local and some provincial soldiers and followed Jiban's detachment.

Captain Thomas saw this and saw also that the majority of the rebel army was escaping. He shouted to Lieutenant Hay:

"With only a few hundred men I can kill these remaining rebels. You take the artillery and the rest of our men and follow the retreating rebel army. Lieutenant Watson is attacking from the left. You attack from the right. But see to it that you reach and block the way to the bridge first. Thus surrounded the rebels can be slaughtered like rats in a trap. They are quick-footed Indian soldiers. Above all, they are experts in retreating. You may find it difficult to overtake them, so rush our cavalry to the gate of the bridge. If you do this, the day is ours."

Lieutenant Hay carried out the orders of Captain Thomas scrupulously.

Pride has disgrace for its reward. In his utter contempt for the rebel soldiers, Captain Thomas retained only a few hundred infantry to fight against Bhavan, sending all the guns and the rest of his men with Lieutenant Hay.

Clever Bhavan was quick to notice that all the cannon and most of the soldiers were removed from his sector. He knew he could easily crush the handful of men under Captain Thomas.

"Children," Bhavan shouted joyously, "we shall kill these few English soldiers immediately for I must rush to the aid of Jiban. So sing the *Bande Mataram.*

The Children sang the *Bande Mataram* and fell upon the Captain's detachment with such force that they were all killed. The Captain himself, however, fought to the last. Bhavan rushed to the Captain, caught him by the hair and said:

"Captain Thomas, I won't kill you. You are too despicable to kill. But you are my captive."

Captain Thomas tried to lift his rifle to kill his captor, but Bhavan seized him fiercely. The Englishman could not move an inch. He was utterly helpless.

"Tie this English rogue tight," Bhavan said to his attendants. "Then place him on a horse. Now we must rush to the help of Jiban. We'll take the captive English captain along with us."

Captain Thomas was tied up securely and placed on a horse. And the handful of Children under the leadership of Bhavan, singing the *Bande Mataram*, marched towards the contingent of Lieutenant Watson.

At the retreat, the discouraged soldiers under Jiban had become further demoralized. They showed the utmost anxiety to run away. Both Jiban and Dhiren had to use all their power of persuasion to keep them intact. And yet many Children escaped into the shelter of mango groves. Jiban and Dhiren led the rest of their soldiers to the mouth of the bridge. But there they were surrounded by the detachments of both Hay and Watson. All hope of escape then vanished. Ruin seemed to embrace them.

Chapter 11

By this time the English guns had reached the battlefield to the right. The Children were utterly demoralized and hopelessly scattered, without the least hope of escape. Jiban and Dhiren failed in their efforts to rally them into a fighting force.

"Go to the bridge, go to the bridge" some one shouted loudly. "And then cross the bridge. Otherwise you all will drown in the river. Face the English soldiers and then slowly walk backward to the bridge."

Jiban found Bhavan in front of him.

"Jiban," Bhavan said, "take them all to the bridge. We are doomed, for sure."

The soldiers of the Mother slowly withdrew to the bridge. But as crowds got on the bridge, they became merely a splendid target for the British guns. Hundreds more thus met their death. Bhavan, Jiban and Dhiren consulted together and discovered that one particular piece of English artillery was most effective in killing the Children.

"Jiban and Dhiren draw your swords; let us capture that cannon," said Bhavan.

With the utmost bravery, the three heroes soon succeeded in killing the artillerymen behind the cannon. Then other Children came to their help. Bhavan captured the cannon. He jumped on it, clapped his hands and shouted:

"*Bande Mataram!* Jiban, let us turn this gun around, and reduce the English troops to atoms."

The Children quickly manned the cannon and turned it around. And the gun poured forth volley after volley with deadly precision. Many English soldiers were killed. Bhavan then placed the cannon at the mouth of the bridge and said:

"Jiban and Dhiren, you two lead our soldiers across the bridge. I alone shall guard and protect it. Leave only a few artillerymen with me."

Twenty gunners stayed with Bhavan.

Under the leadership of Jiban and Dhiren thousands of Children marching in rows, crossed over to the other bank of the river. And Bhavan, with the help of his twenty artillerymen, continued mowing down the English army. But the English troops seemed inexhaustible, and in waves they pressed forward. Bhavan was hard-pressed and harassed; but he stood his ground untiring, unconquered, and fearless.

Baffled, the English soldiers attacked him with renewed vigor, as if with the force of waves lashed by a fierce cyclone. But Bhavan and his twenty comrades stood fast, blocking the entrance to the bridge. They seemed to have defied defeat and to have conquered death itself—crushing the hope of the English to pursue the retreating Children. In the meantime, a majority of the Children had crossed the bridge. A few more minutes of heroic defense and all the remaining patriots would be out of danger on the opposite bank of the river.

Suddenly, as if out of the sky, new guns thundered. Both sides stopped fighting for a moment to find out where these new cannon could be. Then they saw them emerging from the forests, led by India's soldiers. Once out of the woods, seventeen new pieces began to open merciless fire on the English soldiers under Lieutenant Hay. The terrific noise shook the forest and the mountains to their very foundations. The English troops, weary after a day's fighting, wavered at this sudden call of death, and immediately started running for their lives. Only a few English soldiers died facing these new weapons. Bhavan was fiercely excited.

"Look, there run the soldiers of the English army!" said Bhavan. "Comrades, let us pursue them."

The Children from the other side of the River began to rush back to join in a new attack on the English forces. They attacked with such uncanny skill that the English had not even a chance to fight back but were simply carried on the crest of the Children's heroic fury. The enemy soon discovered that behind them was the infantry of Bhavan, and in front were the guns of Mahendra Singh of Padachina. Lieutenant Hay faced total destruction. Neither his strength nor energy, neither his courage nor skill, neither his training nor pride were of any avail. Almost all his soldiers lay dead on the ground, drenched in their own blood. At last the English artillerymen too began to run away. Jiban and Dhiren pursued them with shouts of—"Kill them, kill them." And the Children quickly captured their cannon. Countless English soldiers and Indian sepoys perished. To save their own lives, Lieutenants Hay and Watson sent this message to Bhavan:

"We are all willing to be taken captive now. Please do not slaughter us further."

Jiban looked at Bhavan. Bhavan thought within himself:

"That won't do, brother, that will never do—I have to die today. I must and I will die today—yes, die to make atonement for—"

He waved his sword, shouted *Bande Mataram*, and ordered:

"Kill the enemy, kill the English soldiers. Long live the English people! But kill the English soldiers in India! They are traitors alike to England, India and Humanity!"

Hardly a man of the English army was to be found alive. But at last Bhavan discovered twenty or thirty English soldiers gathered in a corner. They had determined to die fighting; so, with their backs against the wall, they began to defend themselves.

"Bhavan," Jiban said, "we have won the battle. Please cease fighting. None but these few of the British are alive on the battlefield! Let us grant these men their lives and return."

"I shall not return, ever," Bhavan retorted, "as long as one of these Englishmen remains alive. Jiban, I beg you, retire from here and watch from a distance how I alone shall slaughter these English enemies of our beloved Mother India; for I must die today—and I will die today—yes, die to—"

Captain Thomas was still tied on the horse. Bhavan ordered:

"Place that Thomas before me. He must die before I do."

Captain Thomas understood Bengali, so he said to the English soldiers:

"Englishmen, I shall presently die. Please uphold the glory of old England. For Christ's sake kill me first, and then kill the rebels."

An English soldier lost no time in shooting the English captain through the head and the proud officer died instantly.

"Well," Bhavan said, "I am thus cheated of my prey. But who can protect me now? Look, the English soldiers are falling upon me like so many wounded tigers. I have come here to die today. Come, who else of the Children will die with me!"

Dhiren stepped forward first, followed by Jiban. And they were attended by about fifty others. Bhavan looked at Dhiren and said:

"Are you coming to die with us too?"

"Why, is death the monopoly of anyone in particular?" And Dhiren at once proceeded to wound an Englishman.

"No, I don't mean that. But if you die, how can you spend the rest of your days in the company of your wife and children?"

"Are you talking of last night's incident? I am really surprised that you have not understood it yet!" And Dhiren killed the Englishman.

"No," said Bhavan, whose right arm was cut off just then by an English sabre.

"Do you think I myself would have dared to speak of those things to a pure-hearted patriot like you? Mahatma Satya, our Master, sent me as his agent to try you out."

"Why so? What! Is it possible that my Master lost faith in me?" Bhavan asked, fighting with but one arm.

"Yesterday our Master heard with his own ears your entire conversation with Kalyani," said Dhiren as he fought to protect Bhavan.

"How is that possible?"

"He himself was present there. He was teaching the *Gita* to Kalyani when you arrived. Look out, Bhavan, fight carefully." And Bhavan's other arm was cut off.

"Please tell Master Satya of my death and assure him that I am no traitor."

"He knows that, he knows that," Dhiren said with tears in his eyes, as he continued fighting the English soldiers. "Remember the voice and the words of his blessing last night. And he told me today: 'Please stay near Bhavan. He is to die today. Please tell him at his death that I bless him; and that he is sure to attain heaven after death!' "

"Victory to the Children, victory to thee all. Brother Dhiren, please sing the *Bande Mataram* at my death. I want to die with it ringing in my ears."

At the command of Dhiren, the infuriated Children sang the *Bande Mataram* with all the force and all the feeling at their command. The song vitalized their arms and hearts with renewed strength. The last of the English soldiers were killed by the patriots of India—the heroic Children of Mother India. The battlefield became quiet as a graveyard.

At that moment with his mind fixed on the Infinite and with *Bande Mataram* on his lips and in his ears, Bhavan fell dead.

Chapter 12

THE victorious Children celebrated their victory on the banks of the Ajai. Mahatma Satya was the center of attraction. Crowds gathered around him in joyous and demonstrative festivities. But the Mahatma was sad at heart. He was thinking of Bhavan.

During the battle the Children had had little music. But somehow or other hundreds of wind and leather instruments managed to arrive at the Ajai to swell the tide of merrymaking with deafening sound. The festivities continued for a long time.

"God has indeed been kind to the Children," Mahatma Satya said. "But there is one thing that still remains unfinished. We cannot afford to forget those who have made these festivities possible; and yet, they are not here to enjoy them with us. Let us cremate those dead lying on the battlefield. Especially, let us cremate the dead body of Bhavan with proper honors; for that great soul won this victory for us and gave his very life to win it for the Mother."

They lighted a fire of sandal wood, and cremated Bhavan's dead body with highest honors singing the *Bande Mataram* from the very depth of their souls.

After the cremation, Mahatma Satya, Jiban, Mahendra, Nabin and Dhiren met in the woods for a secret conference.

"The cause," Mahatma Satya said, "for which we have so long sacrificed our homes, our hearts, our professions, our personal duties, and all sources of earthly happiness, is now crowned with success. The British are driven out of this part of our country. Their soldiers are gone and the few that are left will soon be crushed by us. What do you think we should do now?"

"Let us march out of here and capture the capital and drive the British beyond the seas," said Jiban.

"I, too, think the same way," Mahatma Satya said.

"Where are the soldiers for that?" Dhiren inquired.

"Why, there are plenty of soldiers around!" Jiban said.

"Whom do you mean?" Dhiren asked.

"They are resting here. When the war drums beat they will all rally round us," Jiban said.

"You would not find a soul to respond to your call."

"Why?" the Mahatma inquired.

"They are all away looting," Dhiren said. "The villages are now unprotected. They are going to loot the English silk factories before they return home. You will not find any one now. I went out to look for them."

"When all is said and done," Mahatma Satya said sadly, "we have captured this part of the country. There is no one here to question our sovereignty. You may establish our kingdom here, gather taxes and revenues from the people, and then recruit soldiers to occupy the capital and free all India from Kashmere to Cape Comorin. When we establish our independent kingdom, the very news of it will win us the allegiance of our fellow-countrymen in the distant provinces and states."

They all bowed at the Mahatma's feet.

"Master," Jiban said, "we bow before you. Master, if you so desire, we shall build a throne for you here."

For the first time in many years Mahatma Satya showed anger and said:

"Shame on all of you. Do you think I am such an empty headed person? None of us may be king. We all are ascetics. The king of the country is God himself. He is our Protector. After we capture the capital, you may crown a king. But know this for certain that I shall accept no other duty in life except the one of rigid asceticism. You may now retire to your respective duties."

The four Children saluted the Mahatma, and were about to retire. Quite unnoticed by others, Satya signalled Mahendra to stay.

"Mahendra," the Mahatma said, "all of you took the oath before the golden map of Mother India. Both Bhavan and Jiban broke their oaths of honor. Bhavan made proper atonement with his life today. I am afraid some of these days Jiban, too, will follow him. But I cling to one ray of hope that for a certain mysterious reason he may not die yet. You, however, are the only one who has been truly loyal to his vow. Now we have reached our temporary goal. You promised not to see your wife and child until we had won success. Now we are successful. You may return home to be a householder again."

"Master, how can I be a householder again?" said Mahendra, crying like a child. "My wife committed suicide and I do not know where my daughter is. And how can I ever expect to know where to look for her now? You once told me that she was alive but that is all I know of her."

Then Mahatma Satya asked Nabin to return to him and be introduced to Mahendra:

"This is Nabin, my pure and beloved disciple. He will tell you all about your daughter," and the Mahatma signalled a message to Nabin. Nabin bowed to the Mahatma and was about to retire when Mahendra inquired:

"Where and when shall I meet you, Nabin?"

"Please, come to my cottage," said Nabin, and led the way.

Mahendra bowed at the Mahatma's feet and followed Nabin to her cottage. It was late at night. Nabin refused to rest. She at once started for the city alone.

Book 4

Chapter 1

THE night of the great victory was a night of revelry. The Children went wild with the chanting of *Bande Mataram*. Some robbed the dead enemies of their weapons, and others seized their jewels and money. Some rushed towards the village and others towards the city. Under penalty of death the Children forced travelers and householders alike to shout *Bande Mataram*. Some looted candy shops for pastry and sweets, others the dairy shops for milk and butter.

The city and the villages became furious with excitement. The British had been defeated in battle! The Hindusthanee loyalists had been defeated most ignominiously on all sides. The patriots set fire to the homes of the loyalists and harassed them in so many ways that they hurriedly left the villages and rushed to the city. The Children handled the pro-British roughly wherever they found them. Everywhere the British were in danger. They were assaulted at sight. Their homes, shops and factories were burnt to ashes.

News of the victory of the Children spread far and wide. Men, women and children, the old, the young and the invalid heard of it. Kalyani was joyous to learn of this triumph of her husband. She thought:

"Dear God, today your cause has met with success. I must start tonight in quest of my husband. Oh, most merciful God, I beg you to help me."

She rose from her bed at midnight. Opening a window of her room she looked about. No one was to be seen in the bylane. So she left the house and began to walk along the public road. Again she prayed:

"My God, my God, may I meet my husband tonight at Padachina."

When she reached the city gate, a guard asked:

"Who goes there?"

"I am a woman," replied Kalyani, a little frightened.

"You are not allowed to pass."

The Chief of the guards heard this and said, "There is no objection to anyone going out, but no one can come in."

So the guard said to Kalyani:

"Go, mother, there is no objection to your going, but it is dangerous for you to go forth on a night like this. I do not know what might happen to you. You may be robbed or you may die in a ditch. You should not go out at a time like this."

"Dear brother," Kalyani said, "I am only a beggar woman. I have not even a penny with me. How can robbers molest me?"

"My little mother, you are young and beautiful.

That is the greatest asset on earth. At the least hint from you I could turn robber myself this very moment."

Kalyani quite understood; but she pretended ignorance and said not a word. The guard, much disappointed at this apparent lack of humor on her part, began to smoke his pipe of hemp.

Kalyani silently walked away.

That night the public streets were infested by rowdies. Some shouted, "Beat him up," and others, "Run away, run away." Some were crying and others laughing. Everybody was suspicious of everyone else. Kalyani found herself in great difficulty. She forgot the way to Padachina; and she could not ask any one, for all were in a fighting mood. Stealthily she made her way onward, walking only in the dark. Even so, she suddenly fell into the hands of a group of the wildest rebels, who shouted aloud to find such a prey, and rushed to catch hold of her. Kalyani ran as fast as she could, and escaped into a forest. Two men followed her even there. One caught her by the flying hem of her *sari* and cried, "My darling, O my darling!"

But another quickly rushed to the scene and struck the rogue with a stick. Wounded, the villain fell back. The man who came to Kalyani's rescue was dressed as a *sanyasi*. He was young. He said to Kalyani:

"Please, do not be afraid any more. Come with me; and tell me where you want to go."

"I want to go to Padachina," Kalyani said.

The holyman, surprised to hear this, said: "What do you mean? Do you really want to go to Padachina?"

And the *sanyasi* placed his hands on Kalyani's shoulders and scrutinized her face intently in the darkness.

At this bold touch of a man, Kalyani was both afraid and angry. Tears rushed to her large eyes. She was almost paralyzed with fear. It was even beyond her power to try to run away. Suddenly the holyman whispered:

"I know who you are. You are our naughty little Kalyani."

Kalyani was still more afraid at hearing such endearing terms from a holyman, and asked:

"Who are you?"

"I am your slave, Kalyani. Dearest Kalyani, I am your slave. Oh, most beautiful one, won't you honor me with your love?"

Kalyani pulled herself a few steps away from the stranger.

"Did you save my life only to insult me this way?" she said, fire in her eyes and contempt in her voice. "I see you are dressed as a holyman. Does a holyman behave like this? I am helpless here tonight. I cannot defend myself."

"Oh, my best beloved, I have been longing for the warm touch of your divine body."

And the holyman rushed towards her and forcibly embraced her.

Kalyani laughed aloud. She cried most happily:

"You should have told me that you were a woman."

"Sister," Shanti said, "you are looking for Mahendra, I know."

"Who are you? I see you know everything."

"I am a *sanyasini*, a captain in the army of the Children. I am a very heroic person. I do know everything. The highway is very dangerous. You cannot go to Padachina tonight."

Kalyani began to cry.

Shanti rolled her beautiful eyes and said:

"What should we be afraid of? We both can conquer thousands of our enemies with just the romantic glances of our eyes. Come, on second thought, let us go to Padachina."

Kalyani was happy beyond words. She felt as if heaven itself had descended to the palm of her hands to gain the assistance of such a clever woman. She was much comforted and encouraged and she said to the girl clad in the garb of a holyman:

"I trust you, sister, I shall go wherever you take me."

Shanti led her then through a secret path in the woods.

Chapter 2

When Shanti left for the city that night Jiban had been present in the cottage.

"I am going to the city for Kalyani," she said to him. "Please tell Mahendra that his wife is alive."

Jiban had heard the story of Kalyani's revival from Bhavan. He also knew of the present whereabouts of Kalyani from Shanti. And so Jiban told Mahendra everything he knew of Kalyani. At first Mahendra refused to believe him. Then, overpowered with happiness, he felt as if he were in a trance of bliss.

Shanti made it possible for Mahendra to meet Kalyani at the dawn of the next day. Husband and wife met in the serene solitude of the woods and in the dark shadows of the trees before the waking of the beasts and the birds of the jungle. Their meeting was witnessed by the fading stars in the blue sky and the endless rows of sal trees. In the distance, one could hear the music of a little stream as it rippled against rocks and stones. A stray cuckoo occasionally struck an entrancing note. . . .

Later, at about nine o'clock, Jiban came to where Shanti was talking with Kalyani. Kalyani was saying to Shanti:

"Dear sister Shanti, we shall ever remain as your slaves for all you have done for us. Now, please complete your kindness by telling us where we may find our little child."

"I want to sleep a little now," Shanti said to Jiban gently, as she looked at his face imploringly. "I have been on my feet for the last twenty-four hours and have not slept at all for the last two nights—I am human you know."

Kalyani smiled a little. Jiban turned to Mahendra and said:

"I will take care of that. You two may go to Padachina. You will meet your daughter there."

Jiban left for Bharuipur to fetch Sukumari from Nimi. It was no easy task. Nimi was sad at the very idea of parting with Sukumari whom she had been nurturing as her own daughter. Her face went through a thousand tragic changes at the thought of giving up such a sweet child—the child she loved so much. At last she burst into a wail, and said:

"I won't give up Sukumari. I can't, I can't!"

"My dear Nimi," Jiban said, "what makes you cry? Sukumari's parents do not live far away. You can visit them and see the child you have grown so fond of."

"Well, after all, this child belongs to you. Why don't you take her away?" Nimi said. Then she brought

Sukumari out, placed her on Jiban's lap and sat down again to weep.

Jiban was at a loss to know what to say or what to do. So he began to talk of different, unrelated things. Nimi's anger, however, was not appeased. She was furious. Rushing into the house, she brought out and in quick succession threw before her brother bundles of Sukumari's clothes, her jewels, her ribbons, her pins, her dolls and her toys.

Sukumari gathered these together herself, and asked Nimi: "Mother dear, where am I going?"

Nimi could not bear it any longer. She lifted Sukumari to her bosom and ran away sobbing bitterly. Jiban had to struggle hard and long to get the little girl back from Nimi.

Chapter 3

THE new fort at Padachina saw the reunion of Mahendra and Kalyani, Jiban and Shanti, Nimi and Sukumari. It was a happy gathering indeed. Shanti came in the garb of Nabin. The night Shanti escorted Kalyani to the cottage in the woods, she had asked her not to tell Mahendra that Nabin was a woman.

At Padachina Kalyani once asked Nabin to enter the women's quarters—the *zenana*. Despite the protests of the servants, Nabin did.

"Why did you send for me, sister?" Nabin asked Kalyani.

"How long," Kalyani asked, "will you dress as a man? I can t see you. I cannot talk to you. You must reveal your identity to my husband."

Nabin stood pensive; spoke not a word for some time. Then at last she said: "There is much danger in that, Kalyani!"

And they both began to discuss the problem of identity. In the meantime the servants who had tried to stop Nabin from entering the *zenana* reported to Mahendra that a man had entered the *zenana* by force, and against their vehement protests. Suspicion led Mahendra quickly to the *zenana*. He entered Kalyani's bedroom to find Nabin standing there. Kalyani had her arms around Nabin, but actually she was only untying the knots of the tiger skin around Shanti's breast. Mahendra was shocked! He was speechless with furious anger and mortification.

"How is it, Mahendra, that you distrust a comrade Child?" Nabin asked smiling.

"Was Bhavan very trustworthy?"

"Do you think," Nabin said, her eyes twinkling, "that Kalyani ever placed her arms around Bhavan to untie the knots of a tiger skin?" And she caught hold of the hands of Kalyani to stop her from untying the knots any further.

"What do you mean by that?"

"I mean that you may distrust me, but how dare you distrust Kalyani?"

"Why, what makes you think that I distrust Kalyani?" said Mahendra much embarrassed.

"Otherwise, why have you followed me so quickly into Kalyani's room?"

"I have something to tell Kalyani. That's why I am here."

"Then you may go now. I, too, have something to tell Kalyani. You had better go from here. Let me talk to her first. This is your home. You may come in here any time you like. It was difficult for me to come here this once."

Wise Mahendra stood profoundly perplexed. He could not solve the riddle. No guilty man, he thought, ever talked in such a vein. Kalyani, too, behaved strangely. She did not run away like a guilty wife. She was not afraid; nor was she ashamed. Instead, she continued to smile as sweetly as was her wont. How could the same Kalyani who had cheerfully swallowed poison under the tree be such a treacherously faithless wife—such a guilty woman?

Nabin was moved at this predicament of Mahendra. When she smiled and cast a coquettish glance at Kalyani, the riddle was solved automatically. Mahendra realized that such a glance could only be the glance of a woman. Courage made him dare to pull Nabin by the beard. The false beard and moustache fell to the floor. During the excitement Kalyani managed to undo the knots of the tiger skin around Nabin's breast. The tiger skin, too, fell to the floor. Caught red-handed, Shanti blushed and looked down shyly.

"Who are you?" Mahendra asked.

"My name is Nabin," replied Shanti.

"That is a false name. Are you a woman?"

"It seems impossible for me to say no to your question now."

"Then why do you, a woman, keep constant company with Jiban?"

"I prefer not to tell that to you."

"Does Jiban know that you are a woman?"

"Yes, he does."

The pious, dutiful and even punctilious Mahendra was much grieved to hear this.

Kalyani, moved by the sadness on the face of her husband, burst forth: "She is Jiban's wife. Her name is Shanti."

For an instant Mahendra looked cheerful, but then his face darkened again. Kalyani understood the cause and quickly said:

"Shanti observes the strictest laws of the Order of the Children."

Chapter 4

THUS Northern Bengal won her independence from the British and the Children began to rule. They continued to do so for some time. But Warren Hastings was then the British governor-general at Calcutta. He was not a man to yield easily. So he sent a Major Edwards with fresh soldiers to subdue the Children and to put an end to their rule.

Major Edwards discovered before long that his task was far unlike that in a European war. The Children had no standing army, no city, no capital, no fort; yet they ruled supreme over their part of India. The British ruled only over territory where they pitched their tents for the day. Immediately after their departure, that very place would resound with the rebel war-cry of *Bande Mataram*.

Major Edwards could not discover whence the Children came like rows of ants, to burn villages that happened to come under British rule, and to slaughter British soldiers. After a vigorous search, he at last discovered that the rebels had built a fort at Padachina to protect their arsenal, as well as their treasury. He decided to capture that fort, and sent spies to discover the strength of the rebel army guarding it. From the information he gathered, he knew it would not be wise to make a direct attack on the fort of the Children. And so he devised a bit of strategy.

The full-moon day of the wintry month of *Magh* was near at hand. A fair was to be held on the banks of the river not far from the camp of Major Edwards. This year the fair was to be an extraordinary one. Generally about one hundred thousand people came. But this year when the Children became the rulers of the territory, they decided to celebrate the occasion with extra pomp and splendor. There was every possibility that most of the Children would attend the fair in order to celebrate their great victory. Major Edwards also surmised that even the soldiers of Padachina were apt to come to this fair. It would be an opportune time to capture the fort with all its arms, munitions and wealth.

With this in view, he spread the news that he was to attack the fair, and kill all the assembled Children in one place and in one day. He would never allow the Children to have their way. This news spread so from village to village that the Children armed themselves and rushed to the defense of the fair. Most of them reached the fair on the full-moon day. Major Edwards had been absolutely right in his speculations. It was a lucky thing for the British that Mahendra, too, stepped into the trap. He left only a handful of soldiers at Padachina and started for the fair with the rest.

Long before this new development, Jiban and Shanti had left Padachina. There was no talk of a new war then nor were they interested in warfare. They had decided to drown themselves at an auspicious hour of the holy full-moon day of the month of *Magh* to make atonement for Jiban's supreme sin—his broken oath. But on their way to the fair they learned that a terrific battle was about to begin between the Children and the English soldiers assembled there.

"Then let us hurry to the fair," Jiban said to Shanti, "and die fighting for Mother India."

"Yes, indeed, it is the highest form of death," Shanti said, "to die for a righteous cause."

Shanti and Jiban hastened towards the fair. Their road led them to the top of a little hill. From there heroic Shanti discovered, at a little distance below, the encampment of the British army. She looked into the eyes of Jiban and said:

"Let death wait; now say *Bande Mataram*."

Chapter 5

SHANTI and Jiban whispered to each other in consultation. Jiban hid himself inside the jungle. Shanti entered another part of the jungle and there began to engage herself mysteriously.

Shanti was going to die, but she had the desire to die in the dress of a woman, for Mahendra had called her male dress a falsely deceiving one. How could she die in a dress of deceit? She had brought with her a little hand-basket containing all her feminine clothes. She began to change in the jungle. She garbed herself as a mendicant woman, half-covering her face with her hair. Then playing on her *sarengi* she entered the British encampment as a beggar woman. The black-bearded sepoys of the British army became excited at seeing such a charming young female mendicant. They ordered her to sing their favorite songs. Shanti sang them gloriously. Some gave her rice, some coppers, some sweets and others pieces of silver. She studied the British camp very carefully. As she was about to go away, the sepoys asked:

"When are you coming here again?"

"I do not know," she replied. "My home is far away from here."

"How far?"

"My home is at Padachina."

One of the sepoys, knowing that that very day Major Edwards was gathering information about Padachina, brought the mendicant woman to the Captain. The Captain in turn took her to the Major. Shanti smiled flirtatiously at the Major and almost intoxicated him with the ravishing glances of her black eyes; she sang in sanskrit about the destruction of India's enemies with the sword of the Mother.

"Where is your home?" Major Edwards asked.

"My home is at Padachina," Shanti replied quickly.

"Where is that? Is there a fort there?"

"Yes, indeed, a very big fort!"

"How many soldiers are there?"

"Twenty to fifty thousand."

"Nonsense! Only two to four thousand soldiers can stay in a fort. How many are there now? And how many do you think have gone out of the fort?"

"Where could they go to, I wonder?"

"Why, to the fair! When did you leave home?"

"Only yesterday."

"Perhaps they have gone out today."

Shanti, understanding the entire situation, thought within herself: "My life is of no use if I do not annihilate you and your army together. I am anxious to see your head chewed by the jackals of the woods!"

But she spoke out: "Major Sahib, that may be possible. They might have gone out today. I am only a beggar woman. I sing songs and beg for my living. I do not know much about those things. But I do know that I am tired of talking. Please give me a few pennies for I must be gone. Or, if you want to reward me well, I can return the day after tomorrow and let you have all the information you need."

"The day after tomorrow won't do," the Major said as he threw a silver rupee to her, "I must have this information tonight."

"What impudence! You had better go to sleep. Do you think it is possible to make forty miles a day on foot? What a *chucho* of a man!"

"What is a *chucho*?"

"A *chucho* is a hero, a great General," Shanti smiled.

"A great General! Yes, indeed, I may be one myself some day—like Lord Clive, you know. But I must have this information tonight. I offer you one hundred rupees."

"You may offer me a thousand. I cannot possibly travel forty miles on foot in one day."

"How about doing it on horseback?"

"If I knew how to ride on horseback, do you think I would come to your camp and sing songs to beg for a living?"

"How about being carried on a man's lap?"

"On a man's lap? Do you think I have no sense of decency?"

"How absurd! I offer you five hundred rupees cash!"

"Who will go with me? Will you go yourself, Major Sahib?"

Major Edwards pointed at a young English officer, and said: "Lindlay, are you willing to go?"

Lindlay sized up the youth and the beauty of the beggar woman, and said: "With great pleasure!"

The young officer was soon ready with a beautiful Arab horse. He tried to push Shanti up into the saddle.

"Shame on you!" Shanti said. "How can I get on a horse before so many people? Do you think I am altogether shameless? You had better proceed. Let us be away from the crowds first."

Lindlay mounted the horse and walked it slowly. Shanti walked behind. Thus they left the camp and entered a solitary meadow. In an instant Shanti placed her foot on that of Lindlay and jumped on the horse without the least effort.

"I see you are an expert horsewoman!" Lindlay said, laughing with wonder.

"I am such an expert horsewoman," Shanti said, "that I am ashamed to ride with you. Who cares to ride with his feet in the stirrups?"

As a boastful gesture, Lindlay quietly removed his feet from the stirrups. Shanti at once caught the stupid man by his neck and quickly pushed him off the horse. She then took her usual seat and touching the horse with her silver anklets galloped away as fast as the wind. The hapless Lindlay lay prone on the ground.

Chapter 6

MAJOR EDWARDS was a veteran army officer. He had scouts watching at every important center. He soon learned that the beggar woman had thrown Lindlay from his horse and had ridden off with it. On hearing this news, the Major was furious. "An imp of satan! Strike the tents!" he ordered.

Like a city built of clouds the canvas tents disappeared in a few minutes. These were placed on wagons. The cavalrymen mounted their horses and the infantry, mixed soldiers of the British army, fell in with rifles on their shoulders. The artillery began to rumble along the road.

Mahendra had started for the fair with his soldiers. Later that afternoon he decided to encamp for the night. The Children had no tents, so they slept on blankets or burlap pieces spread under the trees. They ate little. Mahendra came by an orchard and there issued the order:

"Let us encamp right here for the night."

Just behind this orchard was a little hill somewhat difficult to climb. Mahendra observing this thought that it might be a better idea to encamp on the hill. He determined to look over the ground on the summit and slowly rode up the hill on his horse. Just then a young man joined the army of the Children and said: "Let us march up the hill, comrades!"

"Why," inquired those who were near him.

The young warrior leaped to a mound of earth and shouted: "Children, march forward! In this beautiful moonlit night fragrant with the perfume of the early blossoms of the spring, we must fight our foes, and fight to win!"

The Children at once realized that it was Jiban who was speaking. They shouted *Bande Mataram* fervently, jumped up, and quickly began to march up the hill under Jiban's leadership. Some one quickly brought a caparisoned horse for him.

Seeing all this from a distance, Mahendra was surprised. He was astonished at this march of his soldiers without command. Turning his horse, he began to ride down the hill like lightning. When he met Jiban he asked: "What joke is this, Jiban?"

"It is a great joke!" Jiban said. "It is a joyous joke indeed! Major Edwards is on the other side of the hill on his way to capture our fort at Padachina. The party that climbs the hill first, wins."

Jiban then thus addressed the Children: "Do you know me, Children? I am Jiban, and I have killed at least one thousand English officers and soldiers."

"We know you. You are our own Jiban," thundered back the Children; and their majestic cry echoed on the hills and through the groves.

"Then shout *Bande Mataram.*"

"*Bande Mataram, Bande Mataram, Bande Mataram,*" shouted the Children.

"The enemy is on the other side of the hill," Jiban said with all the feeling at his command. "The night is beautiful, and the sky is blue; and tonight we must fight. March fast, comrades, march fast. Those who reach the summit first win the battle. So sing *Bande Mataram* and march fast—up the hill, Children, up the hill!"

The hills and the forests resounded with the shouts of *Bande Mataram*. Slowly the Children began the ascent. But soon they were dismayed to see Mahendra rushing down hill frantically blowing a trumpet. In an instant the crest of the hill was covered with cannon, and the artillerymen of the British army stood clear against the blue sky.

The Children sang:

"Mother, hail!
Thou sole creed and wisdom art,
Thou our very mind and heart,
And the life-breath in our bodies.
Thou as strength in arms of men,
Thou as faith in hearts dost reign."

But the fierce roar of the British cannon drowned this great song of the Children. Hundreds of them began to fall, dead or wounded, on the hillside. The British steadily kept up the cannonading with volleys like thunder. Like sheaves of rice before the farmers at harvest time the Children fell, cut to pieces. Both Jiban and Mahendra tried their best to stem the tide of battle but in vain. The Children began to retreat like falling stones from a hilltop. They ran helter-skelter.

The British soldiers shouted triumphantly and pursued the retreating patriots down the hill. With bayonets fixed, they fell upon the Children in waves. In the melee, Jiban met Mahendra for a moment and said: "Everything is finished today! Let us both die here, fighting for our country's independence."

"If we could win this battle by our death," said Mahendra, "Then certainly I would die cheerfully but a hero should never die in vain."

"Well, let me die in vain. I must die on the battlefield," Jiban said. He looked back and shouted:

"Those who want to die singing the *Bande Mataram* follow me."

Many Children moved towards Jiban. But he said to them: "That won't do! That won't do! Swear by the holy names of God and Mother India that you will never retreat."

Those who had advanced, fell back. Jiban shouted again: "Are there none to follow me? Well, then I go alone, I go alone."

Mahendra stood at a little distance. Jiban mounted a fresh horse and spoke to Mahendra: "Brother, tell

Nabin that I am riding to my death, and that I will meet her in the world beyond death."

And heroic Jiban rode fearlessly into the terrific shower of steel. He had a spear in his left hand, a rifle in his right, and *Bande Mataram* on his lips. There was no chance for him to fight. Such reckless display of courage was fruitless. Yet he repeatedly shouted *Bande Mataram*, and entered the lines of the enemy.

"Turn back, my friends," Mahendra said to the retreating Children. "Just once turn back and look at Jiban. You are sure to gain immortality if you but look at him once."

A few Children turned back and watched the superhuman performance of Jiban. At first they were surprised beyond words. Then they said:

"Jiban knows how to die indeed! Why can't we, too, follow him. Come, comrades, let us enter heaven with Jiban."

At this a number of the Children were inspired to turn back. Another group turned to imitate the first batch of patriots. There was an ominous stir within their ranks. Jiban, in the meantime, had penetrated so far into the lines of the enemy that no one could see him any more.

And so it happened that from all over the battlefield the Children noticed that some of their number had turned back to fight. And they all came to the conclusion that perhaps the Children had been victorious and that they were now pursuing the English soldiers. Then they all turned and shouted: "Kill the English soldiers— Kill the enemy;" and defiantly advanced upon the British troops.

The British soldiers, at this sudden move, became confused and frantic; and sepoys began to run away in different directions. Then the Englishmen too, bayonets in their hands, could be seen trying to make their way rapidly to their camp.

Mahendra, searching for the cause of this demoralization of the British, discovered a new army of Children on the top of the hill. They were descending and attacking the English soldiers from behind.

"Children," shouted Mahendra, "look! There flies the flag of Mahatma Satya on the top of the hill! The Mahatma himself is on the battlefield today. Look, countless numbers of our soldiers are on the crest of the hill. Now, let us crush the enemy to atoms from both sides. Look, our comrades have the top of the hill, Children, look!"

Mahendra's army now mustered courage. His soldiers sang the *Bande Mataram*. They began to climb the hill with energy. The English soldiers became panic-stricken.

Mahatma Satya now attacked the center of the English forces with his large army. A terrible battle ensued. As a little fly is crushed into nothingness between two slabs of stone, just so the British army was crushed between the mighty forces under the command of Mahatma Satya and faithful Mahendra. Before long there was not a man left of the English army to convey to Warren Hastings the news of this historic defeat.

Chapter 7

It was the night of the full-moon. The battlefield was quiet again. The terrific noise of horses' hooves, the rattling of gun carriages, the rifle shots and the roar of the cannon were heard no more. The dense veil of smoke that had covered the panorama had disappeared into the blue of the sky. No one shouted; and no one sang the *Bande Mataram*.

There was noise—but the noise was only that of dogs and jackals. Add to this the moans and groans of the wounded. Men lay with broken arms, broken legs, broken ribs and broken heads. Some cried for their mothers, and others for their fathers. Some begged for water; but most of them for death. Hindus and Mohammedans, Buddhists and Sikhs were all huddled together, weltering in blood. The wounded, the dying and the dead, human beings and horses lay on each other in heaps. The night was cold; but the moon was bright, the pulsating moonbeams adding to the ghastliness of the scene. No one dared to visit the battlefield.

And yet, a lonely woman could be seen walking to and fro in this desolate and dreadful place. She had a torch in her hand, for she was searching for some one. With the help of the torch she looked at the face of one corpse and then at the face of another. Wherever she found a dead soldier lying under a horse, she would plant the torch in the ground, pull away the horse with her own hands, and thus reclaim the human corpse. But when she would discover that she had again failed to find the person she sought, she would take up her torch and gently walk on to the next. For several hours she carried on this quest. She looked into every face; but she did not find the face she was so anxiously seeking.

At last she cast the torch aside and threw herself on the blood-stained battleground, corpses all around her, and sobbed as if her heart would break. This was Shanti looking for the body of Jiban.

As she was sobbing and crying, she heard a sweet and kindly voice say to her: "Mother, arise. Please do not cry."

Shanti opened her eyes to see a holy sage of majestic stature standing in the moonlight before her. She stood up reverently. The sage spoke: "Mother, please do not cry. I shall find the body of Jiban for you. Please come with me."

The sage led her to the center of the battlefield. Countless corpses lay there in heaps. The holyman cleared a mound of corpses to unearth a human body. Shanti instantly knew who it was. It was Jiban. Unnumbered wounds covered his body, which was soaked in blood. Shanti began to cry aloud like any other woman.

"Mother, do not cry," said the sage again. "Is Jiban dead? Calm yourself, and examine his body. Feel his pulse first."

"The pulse is not moving at all," Shanti said as she felt it.

"Then feel his heart."

"The heart has ceased to beat. The body is cold."

"Place your fingers before his nostrils, and see if there is any breath left."

"No, none at all."

"Please try again. Now put your fingers into his mouth and see if there is any warmth left."

"I cannot understand," Shanti said hopefully.

The sage touched Jiban's body with his left hand, and said to Shanti: "You are almost paralyzed with anxiety. So you fail to feel the true condition of your husband, but I believe that there is still a little warmth left in his body. Examine him again."

Shanti again pressed Jiban's pulse. It felt as if it were moving faintly. Surprised she placed her hand on his heart and the heart seemed to beat very, very gently. Then she placed her fingers before his nostrils and she could feel a breath af life. And she also felt warmth in his mouth.

"Was there life left in him; or has life come back to him?"

"How can life come back to a dead body, my

mother? Do you think you can carry him to yonder pond? I am a healer. I want to heal him."

Without the least difficulty, Shanti lifted Jiban from the ground.

"Take him to the pond," said the sage, "and wash all the blood from his body. I am going to fetch some medicine for him."

Shanti carried Jiban to the pond and washed him clean. The sage returned soon with ointments of wild herbs and applied them to all the wounds of Jiban's body. Then he repeatedly passed his hands over Jiban. Suddenly Jiban sighed, and sat up. He looked at Shanti's face and asked:

"Who won the battle, Shanti?"

"You won the battle," Shanti said. "But bow to this holyman who–"

But they found no one there. The majestic figure of the healer had mysteriously vanished. There was no one there to bow to; but they could distinctly hear the noise of the revelries of the victorious army of the Children. In the glorious moonlit night, Shanti and Jiban sat on the bright steps of the pond. Such was the healing power of the medicine administered by the holy healer that Jiban felt absolutely well.

"Shanti," Jiban said very gently, "how extraordinary is the effect of the medicine of the sage! I feel no more pain in my body. I am well. How strange that I am fully cured so soon! Where do you want to go now, Shanti? There, there, I hear the noise of our victorious army!"

"We shall go there no more," Shanti said firmly. "We have won the victory for Mother India. This part of the country now belongs to us. We want no reward for doing our duty. So why should we go there?"

"What we have won by force, must be protected with the strength of our arms."

"Mahatma Satya and Mahendra are there to protect our kingdom. You sacrificed your life for the Children in order to make atonement for a sin. The Children have no more claim upon you. We are now dead to them. If they see us now, they are sure to say: 'For fear of atonement with death Jiban hid himself somewhere during the battle. Now he is out to claim a share in our kingdom.' "

"What do you mean, Shanti? Do you think that for fear of public opinion we should refuse to do our duty? My duty is unselfishly to serve the Mother. Let people gossip any way they like. I must continue to serve the cause of our Mother India."

"You have forfeited all your right to do that. For you did sacrifice your life in the Mother's service. If you can serve her again, then where is the atonement? The outstanding part of the atonement is to be fully deprived of all opportunities to serve the Mother. Otherwise, just to sacrifice an insignificant life is not a great thing in itself."

"Shanti, it remains for you to understand the real kernel of the great problems of life. My greatest happiness lies in performing my duty as a Child in the service of the Mother. I must deprive myself of that happiness.

But where shall we go? We certainly could not be happy at home, thus abandoning our Mother's service."

"That is certainly farthest from my mind. We are no longer householders. We shall ever remain ascetics. And we shall ever observe strictest continence. Come, let us travel all over India, visiting the holy places of pilgrimage."

"What shall we do after that?"

"After that? Yes, after that we shall build ourselves a little cottage on the Himalayas. There we shall pass our days in prayer and meditation—in the service of God. We shall ask direct from Him the boons that are best for Mother India and for all her children; and also for Mother Earth and for all her children the world over."

Shanti and Jiban arose from the steps. Hand in hand they walked away. Singing the *Bande Mataram* they soon disappeared out of sight.

বন্দে মাতরম্

Glossary

ASHRAM—hermitage—a religious or spiritual retreat

BANDE MATARAM—Hail Motherland
BOWDI—the wife of one's elder brother
BRAMACHARINI—continent woman

CHARKA—spinning wheel
CHUCHO—small rodent (term of contempt)

DEVA—a deity
DHARMA—sacred duty
DHOTI—a loin cloth used as a man's garment
DHUTRA—the narcotic thornapple

GITA—Hindu holybook
GURDWARA—Sikh temple
GURU—spiritual guide or teacher

HINDUSTHANEE—an inhabitant of Hindusthan—India

JAISTHA—the second month of the summer
JATAS—matted hair

KABA—long robe reaching the feet
KALAI—a legume—pea family
KSHATRYA—the king and warrior caste

LATHIS—bamboo sticks used as clubs

MAGH—the second month of the winter
MAUND—(of rice) about 80 lbs.
MIRJAI—a short coat with short sleeves
MYNA—a bird noted for its mimicry

PANDIT—wise man, scholar
PARIAH—outcast—one who has no caste
PROJAPATI—butterfly—symbol of marriage

SANYASI—a holyman without family ties
SANYASINI—*ibid*, feminine
SARENGI—stringed musical instrument
SARI—woman's draped garment
SEPOY—a soldier of India

VIHARA—Buddhist temple

ZAMINDAR—land-holder
ZENANA—Women's quarters